# IT GIVES ME GREAT PLEASURE

The Complete *Vade Mecum* for

The
Old Time
Music Hall Chairman

by

Your own, Your *very* own

## MR MICHAEL KILGARRIFF

Including
Production Guide
and
Nearly 600 Patter Entries

SAMUEL  FRENCH

LONDON
NEW YORK TORONTO SYDNEY HOLLYWOOD

Copyright © 1972 by Michael Kilgarriff
Copyright © 1986, revised and rewritten, by Michael Kilgarriff
All Rights Reserved

*IT GIVES ME GREAT PLEASURE* is fully protected under the copyright laws of the British Commonwealth, including Canada, the United States of America, and all other countries of the Copyright Union.

ISBN 978-0-573-09036-3

www.samuelfrench.co.uk
www.samuelfrench.com

The introductions and back announcements included in this book may be freely used in performance. However, permission to use any of the songs referred to in this work must be sought from the appropriate source, or, if this is not known, from The Performing Rights Society.

The right of Michael Kilgarriff to be identified as author of this work has been asserted in accordance with Section 77 of the Copyright, Designs and Patents Act 1988.

# PREFACE TO THE FIRST EDITION

Having been involved for many years now in the world of Old Time Music Hall as manager, accompanist, soloist, critic, and above all as producer and Chairman, I began to realize some time ago that many amateur and professional companies often embark on a Music Hall without any knowledge or experience of the genre.

A steadily increasing number of requests for help and advice from friends and strangers alike has led me, therefore, to the compilation of this Production Guide and Chairman's Handbook, representing as it does a distillation of my own notes, records, past programmes and experience.

The Production Guide is not a minutely-detailed, step-by-step set of instructions—Music Hall is much too variable and subjective a concept for this to be practicable or desirable; every entry in the Chairman's patter section has been tried out in performance, and I am sure that any selection you care to make will not disappoint either you or your audience.

Good luck—and have fun.

MICHAEL KILGARRIFF

# PREFACE TO THE SECOND EDITION

Since *It Gives Me Great Pleasure* first appeared in 1972 I have been heartened to hear from so many producers and performers, both amateur and professional, how useful they have found it as a source of help, information and encouragement and above all of inspiration for their own ideas. For this is very much a suggestive publication, if you'll pardon the expression, the intention being to fire the imagination, to suggest a course of procedure rather than to proclaim an *ex cathedra* list of inviolable do's and don't's.

And now my estimable publishers have permitted me in this new edition to update publishers' addresses, to revise the text in the light of a further fifteen years' Music Hall experience, and considerably to expand the Chairman's section.

My four collections of sketches (*Three Melodramas, Three More Melodramas, Music Hall Miscellany* and *Three Comedy Sketches*) may be of value in making up your programmes, and my two volumes of patter routines, monologues and two-handers entitled *Make 'Em Roar* offer more comedy material.

MICHAEL KILGARRIFF<br>
Ealing

*By the same author*

Three Melodramas (French)
Three More Melodramas (French)
Three Comedy Sketches (French)
Music Hall Miscellany (French)
Make 'Em Roar (Vols I and II) (French)
Comic Speeches for All Occasions (Macdonald-Futura)
The Musical Joke Book (Fentone)
Outrageous Doctors' and Nurses' Joke Book (Ward Lock)
1,000 Jokes for Kids (Ward Lock)

# CONTENTS

## PART I  PRODUCTION GUIDE

### Chapter One—First Considerations

| | |
|---|---|
| Apologia | *page* 3 |
| Advertising | 4 |
| The Foyer and Auditorium | 5 |
| Programmes and Song-sheets | 5 |
| House Lights | 6 |
| Stage Lighting | 6 |
| Costumes | 7 |
| Length of Show | 7 |
| Chairman | 8 |
| Music | 9 |
| Microphones | 13 |
| Scenery | 13 |
| Useful Publications | 15 |

### Chapter Two—The Programme Proper

| | |
|---|---|
| Cross-Overs | 17 |
| Barber-Shop Quartets | 17 |
| Duets | 17 |
| Sketches | 18 |
| Mime | 18 |
| Recitations | 19 |
| Song Sources | 19 |
| Scenas | 20 |
| Marching Routines | 22 |
| The Cast | 22 |
| The Comic | 24 |
| Style and Presentation | 26 |
| Constructing the Programme | 29 |
| Alternatives | 39 |
| Coda | 39 |

## Part II  Your Distinguished Chairman

| | |
|---|---:|
| The Role of the Chairman | 43 |
| Introductions for Shows | 48 |
| Audience Participation | 54 |
| Introductions for Band and Pianist | 56 |
| Latecomers | 60 |
| Song-sheets | 62 |
| Introductions for Gentlemen | 66 |
| Exits for Gentlemen | 72 |
| Introductions for Ladies | 76 |
| Exits for Ladies | 81 |
| General Introductions | 84 |
| General Exits | 91 |
| Duet Introductions and Exits | 94 |
| Late Laughs and No Laughs | 96 |
| Scenery Patter | 99 |
| Heckle-Stoppers | 101 |
| Sketches | 106 |
| Intervals and Loyal Toast | 108 |
| Closers for Shows | 111 |
| Fillers | 114 |
| Miscellaneous | 119 |
| Author's Last Word | 126 |
| Index of Song Titles | 127 |

# Part 1
# PRODUCTION GUIDE

CHAPTER ONE
# FIRST CONSIDERATIONS

**Apologia**

The revival of this very popular form of entertainment continues unabated, but I am only too aware that Music Hall production *per se* remains at a sadly low level—as I am also aware that even the most ill-conceived, under-rehearsed and ineptly performed Music Hall can be wildly successful—such is the power of those old songs and so strong is the appeal of this particular diversion. What follows, therefore, may be considered as so much specious guff; I shall nevertheless inflict it on the reader because I am devoted to the Music Hall in all its aspects and don't care to see it sold short.

I also believe in the pursuit of excellence—I don't care if Granny and Uncle Sid *did* love your Music Hall last Christmas: you and I know it was a rotten production, so why not try to improve things this year? True, your audience may not notice the difference, but you and I will know, and that's what matters, isn't it?

Of course, what we refer to as "Old Time Music Hall" today is nothing of the kind; the contemporary version is an idealized impression of late-Victorian "Variety". However, I am not concerned—and neither, I imagine, are you—with historical accuracy. These few inadequate pages deal with the current conception of "Music Hall", so let us be unashamedly commercial and give the public what it expects—Harry Champion numbers, Marie Lloyd numbers, scenas of Cockney Songs and seaside songs, comedy barber-shop quartets, sketches, red-nosed comics, romantic duets, pretty girls and ripe jokes—all presented in a swift-moving revue style with plenty of singable choruses and belly laughs.

But how to mix all these ingredients into a balanced, homogenous whole? And what should the ingredients be? I hope the following précis—for it pretends to be no more than that—will provide some of the answers.

## Advertising

Don't try to put too much on your posters. They should be colourful, clear to read and uncomplicated—and not too "imaginative". Just include the words "Old Time Music Hall" (*not* that abominably coy "Olde Tyme Music Hall") prominently splashed across the centre; across the top will be the name and address of the theatre or venue; the only other essential information is the date, the time, and the prices of admission. And of course, the box-office telephone number.

If you feel your Chairman is well enough known nationally or locally his name can also be included, but don't list all the names of your cast—they won't draw a penny and only clutter up the poster.

If drinking is permitted in the auditorium during the performance, this facility should be well highlighted on your posters, since this is an amenity which will pull 'em in far more than Betty Blinkers, the pride of Miss Sicklefoot's Dancing and Deportment Academy and winner of the first prize for elocution in her age group at the Birmingstonehamptonthwaite Annual Competitive Music Festival, ever could.

More detailed posters can be placed outside the theatre itself, giving the full cast and any special features of the performance, such as a sketch or speciality act. The cast can be listed with cod bill-matter, i.e.:

| Miss Ada Alpha | Mr Joe Soap |
|---|---|
| Queen Of All She Surveys | Late of the Post Office Rifles |
| Pretty As A Picture | The Beau Brummel Of Song |
| Refined Roguishness | The Wonder Of The Age |
| Ravishing The Senses | In A Class Of His Own |
| Queen Of The Halls | The Immense Favourite |
| Carrying All Before Her | Once Seen Never Forgotten |
| The Vital Spark | Tall And In The Dark |
| Vocaliste Supreme | Handsome |
| The Pocket Venus | Good's Not The Word |
| Our Heart's Delight | Fast And Furious |
| Naughty But Nice | The Furtive Funster |
| Small But Beautifully Marked | Fairly Talented |
| The Pride of (*Local*) | Despite Popular Demand |
| The (*Local*) Nightingale | Society Entertainer |
| | The Bashful Limit |

*Production Guide* 5

Other suggestions for male or female: Multum In Parvo, The Hit Of The Season, Strange But True, Late Opera House Sark, Of Ever-Widening Fame, The Borderline Case, The Viceroy Of Versatility, The (*Local*) Sensation, Sauce And Sparkle, Idol Of The Halls, The Heart-Throb Of The Halls.

Photographs should only be displayed if the artistes are in period costume—modern dress pictures to advertise a period show look so half-hearted.

**The Foyer and Auditorium**

In the foyer you can pin up some of the many period posters which are obtainable from trendy shops; plus some old prints, Union Flags, aspidistras on stands, a barrel-organ and/or honky-tonk pianist (live), a cockle-and-whelk stall, etc., etc. The box-office staff, bar staff and usherettes can be dressed in costume, and card moustaches (from Barnum's of Hammersmith) can be handed to each male member of the audience with his programme.

A large picture of Queen Victoria displayed in a prominent place in the auditorium is a very evocative prop and can be a great help to the Chairman for his Loyal Toast routine, when it should be covered by the follow-spot.

If at all possible and practicable, organize a bar and tables and chairs in the auditorium. This may reduce the size of your audience but you will more than make it up in profits on the drinks. Light snacks are enormous money-spinners; and if the organization (or an outside caterer) will run to it, offer hot meals of a Victorian flavour—saveloys, bangers and mash, pease pudding and so on. And don't forget to provide tea and coffee and soft drinks for the children and the teetotallers.

**Programmes and Song-sheets**

I would strongly advise against any attempt to list the running-order of your show in the programmes—you are bound to cut it or rearrange it. I have twice completely reversed the second and third "halves" of a production of mine and greatly improved the audience response to both. Just list the cast (in alphabetical order, with the ladies first), the musicians and the stage-management. All names should be prefixed with the appropriate title of Miss or Mr; the wardrobe mistress and any other member of the staff to whom the title belongs may be Mrs, and the musical director will always be dignified with the title of Maestro—if a lady, Madame. If your speciality act is a conjurer, he can perhaps be raised to the status of "Professor".

Where finance and facilities allow, a suitably nostalgia-inducing front cover should be designed, and your advertisers asked to provide appropriate period copy and typefaces.

Finally, it is essential for each song on the sheet to be numbered, preferably in show sequence.

## House Lights

The house lights are an important part of Music Hall; bringing them up at regular intervals helps to break down the barrier between stage and audience caused by the footlights and proscenium arch. They should be raised to $\frac{1}{3}$ or $\frac{1}{2}$ for the chorus songs whenever the song-sheets are to be used, for the Loyal Toast, and for any untoward happenings (such as late-comers) to which the Chairman wishes to draw attention.

If the house lights are not controlled from the electrician's board, the operator must be provided with a detailed and comprehensive plot, and he should attend at least the final run-through and dress-rehearsal to make sure that he knows what is going on.

## Stage Lighting

The stage lighting must be as bright as possible, and full up virtually all the time—I have produced many a very successful show with no lighting changes at all. Throw out all those deep reds and blues and substitute straws, pinks and golds. So often I have sat through a drearily underlit show because the producer has tried to be too clever with too little lighting at his disposal, and a gradual atmosphere of gloom has pervaded the house, effectively deadening any attempts at jollity by the cast.

Angle one lamp to cover the Chairman's position: his prominence in the show demands that he be clearly visible—although this lamp will be killed during items after his pronouncements.

Have a follow-spot if you can run to it—or even two—and these will cover up many deficiencies in the number, strength and positioning of lamps. Follow-spots are not so simple to operate as might be imagined—again your operator must attend a few rehearsals and be supplied with a plot. He need only have three "gellies": pink for the ladies, gold or straw for the men, and green for the villain in the sketch, only to be used momentarily for his first entrance.

If you decide to take the lights down for a number, bring them up to full for the final four bars—or down to a black-out and then, after four seconds, bring them up to full for the calls. If you have dimmers, save a little lighting for your grand spectacular finale to a scena, i.e. for the final massed knees-up chorus set the lights at 9, bringing everything up to 10 for the final couple of bars.

But if you haven't got the facilities—or if your electrician is unco-operative or inexperienced—keep it simple; an audience won't notice the lack of intricate lighting effects, but they will notice if they can't see what is going on.

**Costumes**

As with the lighting, these should be as bright and gay as possible. Resist black for the ladies, much as the dears seem to like wearing this mournful colour, and smother them in costume jewellery. Brightly coloured chokers and breast-pocket handkerchiefs for the men can help to lighten a drab suit. A few inches of lace tacked on here and there (such as in the cuffs of the men's dress suits), parasols, flowered hats or head trimmings, lace gloves; canes, boaters and button-holes for the men—these are simple enough touches to give a costume a finished-off look.

And don't forget to provide your orchestra with costumes, also —even if only for their top halves!

**Length of Show**

Music Hall is essentially a trivial form of entertainment, and so I believe that two hours ten minutes or two hours fifteen minutes is quite long enough. I am also in favour of having only one interval of fifteen minutes, although I appreciate that two intervals mean more bar takings which may be vital to the theatre or the company presenting the show.

For a one-interval show, the first half can run a little over the hour and the second a little less; for a two-interval show (with intervals of ten minutes each) I would recommend the first "half" to be the shortest and to run for thirty-five minutes, with the other two halves lasting about forty minutes.

The three-hour show can stretch an audience's patience and goodwill dangerously thin, and the last quarter of an hour will be punctuated by the sound of seats tipping up as people leave to catch their last buses.

Remember the old adage—leave 'em wanting more.

## Chairman

This august personage is the lynch-pin of your Music Hall: he embodies the whole spirit of what we fondly imagine to be the "Good Old Days". The novelty of his period dress, his use of the gavel, his presence throughout the entire performance, his archaic mode of speech with his grave hyperboles and ridiculous introductions—these are his advantages over the modern cabaret's M.C.

He should possess a strong, authoritative personality, laced with an awareness of his own occasional absurdity, and should have a "superabundance of that indefinable quality—charm". He must not be allowed to become self-indulgent and to prattle on and on . . . as I have said, he is on stage for the whole evening, and if his various pronouncements are inordinately protracted your audience will soon be rendered insensible with boredom. A Chairman suffering from verbal diarrhoea can totally upset a carefully arranged programme—after all, you will have planned for the acts to follow each other in a balanced sequence, and if your Chairman does a ten-minute patter turn between each your whole scheme will be rendered at naught.

Lightness is all for the Chairman, but whatever he says and does should never detract from his dignity, however foolish the comics may try to make him, and no matter how much the girls may vamp him. If he takes part in a sketch or scena, his participation should be in character. As Chairman I once went off and changed into boater, blazer and white ducks to perform "*Honeysuckle And The Bee*" in a comedy duet with the delicious Anna Dawson as part of a scena. A producer friend of mine felt this to be a lessening of the Chairman's authority, and on reflection I think he was probably correct. We did get a lot of laughs, but it wasn't *right*.

I have started each chapter in Part II with what I hope are

## Production Guide

helpful hints, do's and don't's for the Chairman. The producer might find them worth a glance or two also, since they contain many observations affecting aspects of Music Hall outside the Chairman's direct sphere of participation. I have also included the correct pronunciation of the word "scena", so Part II is worth reading if only for that.

### Music

Before this section becomes complicated, I should say right at the start that a good solo pianist provides a perfectly adequate accompaniment for a Music Hall. He or she may also be asked to be responsible for the vocal arrangements in the duets, quartets, scenas, and so on—and to choose the right keys for the soloists.

A well-tried old dodge is to raise the final chorus of a song up a semi-tone or a tone to give the ending an extra lift—but make sure this doesn't take the number out of the singer's or the audience's range. The penultimate chorus can sometimes be sung *pianissimo* with the lights checked down—full up and *fortissimo* for the last chorus. A slow number can sometimes be given a strong finish by adding a coda to the last chorus, i.e. be repeating the final four or eight bars; for a fast number by repeating the fifth and sixth bars from the end three times. And don't forget that old stand-by:

> Tiddle-iddle-*a*-da,
> Tiddle-iddle-*a*-da,
> Pom-tiddley-om-pom—Pom! Pom!

This is often used to end a Harry Champion or fast patter song.

"Get-on" bars must be discussed and rehearsed with the pianist; also of course the play-off music, especially if the artiste has a long way to travel to the stage.

Early recordings show that the old Music Hall artistes often ploughed relentlessly through all the verses and choruses of a song without varying the tempo. In some numbers this may be acceptable but in my experience most songs benefit from having the verses sung *Colla Voce*, i.e. freely, with the tempo picked up for each chorus, this gives the performance variety and the singer the chance to point the lyrics clearly.

For scenas I always write out the whole medley in manuscript. The melody line with chord symbols under the stave is quite sufficient for an experienced pianist (indeed professional pianists prefer it) and it saves all that turning back and forth and frantic hurling of sheets to the floor. Never stick sheets of manuscript together with transparent tape since this causes the pages to close of their own volition; use brown sticky paper instead.

If gags are told between verses of a song, the pianist should keep a vamp going and come up from pianissimo to mezzo-forte on the tag line, dropping back to pianissimo if there are more gags to follow. But if there are a number of gags he should stop the vamp and pick it up again on the tag of the final gag or the vamp will become intrusive.

The National Anthem was only used for special occasions prior to the First World War, so I would omit it unless you feel this is likely to give offence, as may be the case with some "maintained" civic theatres.

For chorus singing the pianist should play the melody in octaves well up into the treble range of the piano; this brings out the melody and encourages the audience to sing up.

If your budget will run to more than a pianist, I would advise that your second musician should be a trumpeter and not, as is usually the case, a drummer. To my ears there are few more doleful sounds than the combination of piano and traps, whereas a trumpet gives a bright, cheerful and penetrating sound which can blast out the melody where needed leaving the pianist to provide the rhythm. Also, a trumpet can use three different types of mute to provide changes in tone colour, and most players of this instrument also play the cornet, giving yet another tonal quality.

If your pianist is not used to writing for trumpet, a half-hour with a player will tell him all he needs to know (for Music Hall at least!); the only difficulty lies in the fact that the trumpet is a transposing instrument and requires its score to be written a tone up in relation to the piano. Avoid extreme keys—for instance, if the piano part is in E, the trumpet part will have to be in F sharp, which is a virtually impossible key to play; in this case the piano part would need to be taken down a semi-tone, putting the trumpet into the much more manageable key of F.

All scores, by the way, should have each item numbered consecutively right through the show; with subdivisions within turns or scenas lettered in sequence. For instance the overture will be number 1, the Chairman's chorus will be number 2, and the opening scena will be number 3a, 3b, 3c, and so on through to the audience play-out at the very end of the evening. This saves a good deal of time and confusion at band calls—and don't forget to provide your musical director with a *music* running-order numbered as suggested above.

For a third musician, should you be fortunate enough to be able to afford one, I strongly recommend a trombonist. The trombone is a marvellous instrument for Music Hall, being versatile enough to play a soothing melody as sweetly as you could wish (it can also be muted), and to play those gorgeous rasping glissandi—plus, as a bonus, fruity bass notes for rhythm support when needed.

This is not a difficult instrument to write for, since it is written normally in the bass clef and is not transposing. The only problem might be the upper notes (those above, say, E above middle C) which if they continue for more than a phrase or two are usually written in the tenor clef. But fluency in this clef is soon acquired—I once started scoring a complete show for piano, clarinet doubling flute and trombone, being totally unfamiliar with the tenor clef. Before I was half-way through I was reading and writing it as easily as the treble and bass clefs.

That combination of clarinet/flute and trombone was suggested to me by a musician friend, and proved to be very effective in a small hall—as is the clarinet/flute and trumpet combination. But in a larger hall, or one where the audience may tend to become rowdy, the clarinet and flute just will not be heard—my flautist played almost his entire part on the piccolo in a vain attempt to be heard above the racket! So now I use piano, trumpet and trombone, which for a three-piece band I think is the ideal.

A producer of my acquaintance once used a string trio—piano, violin and cello. He told me when I queried the wisdom of this that he wanted a "Palm Court" atmosphere . . . this he certainly got, and pretty dull it was, too. Not that I am against strings—you may find a brass player who doubles on violin in which case by all means utilize it for the quieter numbers (though this may involve you in an extra fee)—but not at the expense of a trumpet or trombone.

King Palmer's *Teach Yourself Orchestration* (English Universities Press Ltd, 1964) is sufficiently informative without being too detailed, but for the inexperienced scorer, I would advise him to write for brass only for the choruses, leaving the piano to accompany the verses solo and bringing the brass in just on the last bar or two before the refrain. But the brass must be well in evidence, of course, for intros. and play-offs. Not that you have to use your trumpet and trombone for every musical item—if your soprano is singing "*One Fine Day*", I would leave it to the piano.

And where do you find your brass players? The Salvation Army have helped me out in this respect on more than one occasion—their bandsmen are excellent players and experienced sight-readers, which is essential.

Always ensure that the band has copies of "*Happy Birthday*" and "*Twenty-One Today*" (E.M.I.—Feldman's List) to hand; if your Chairman is asked to announce either of these events it looks a bit silly if the audience has to sing without accompaniment.

The overture for the show should consist of three well-known choruses not featured in the programme proper, and in contrasting tempi, e.g. "*Where Did You Get That Hat?*", "*In The Good Old Summer Time*" and "*Hello! Hello! Who's Your Lady Friend?*" Thus you achieve a balance of 2/4, 3/4 and finally 6/8—the rhythm being exactly like that of starting up your car: a snappy get-away in first gear, a leisurely change into second, and then into top gear for the real speed.

I believe in a play-out not only for the acts but for the intervals, which again can be a gentle 3/4 chorus such as "*Comrades*". After the interval, play the house back from the bars with an entr'acte—this, I think, should also be a chorus ("*Here We Are Again*" is ideal), since the audience will begin to sing and re-establish its senses of camaraderie. At the very end of the show, after the encores, the speeches and the final curtain, the poor audience will feel very deflated if the stage-lights go out and the orchestra disappears while they are still getting their hats and coats on. Your footlights at least should stay on for the play-out music: I generally use "*Moonstruck*" from Lionel Monckton's "*Our Miss Gibbs*" (Chappell's) which is not strictly a Music Hall song, but which is bright and jolly, and no-one ever knows the words so the audience is not tempted to hang about and sing.

If your pianist would like assistance with music turnovers, press-gang a wife or girl-friend into service. A slight ability to read music is a help—my wife has helped me in this respect on occasions—but not essential. She should be dressed in costume and precede the pianist into the pit—the Chairman, of course, can make capital out of her presence.

The pianist or M.D. should be supplied with a lighted taper, for it is his task to light the Chairman's candle (the geography of the theatre permitting) and his own immediately before the overture. At the interval he blows the candle out and relights again before the entr'acte. He really does work very hard indeed. . . .

**Microphones**

The use of microphones presents an insoluble problem. They were not in general use until the late twenties and so are out of place in a show purporting to be taking place in the late Victorian or Edwardian era. But the most important thing is for your Music Hall to be *heard*, which is why whenever I am presenting a show at any venue which is not a purpose-built theatre (and sometimes even then) such as a ballroom, a club, exhibition-hall or ship's lounge, I always use the wretched instruments.

I try to organize four mikes: one for the Chairman which is detachable from its stand and is on a long lead so that he can move about, one for the down centre position and the other two on either side from four to six feet apart, depending on the width of the stage. Their great disadvantage is that they tend to inhibit freedom of movement by the artistes, but as I have said, it is better to be a little restricted in this respect than not to be heard.

Remember when testing microphones before a show that an empty hall reverberates; an audience deadens sound to a very marked degree, so the mikes will need to be set a couple of points higher than may at first be apparent. Ideally they should be controlled from the front—and the Chairman should have a switch on his so that he can turn it off when he puts it down on his table, avoiding nasty bumps through the loud-speakers throughout the show.

Microphones are, I know, horrible things, but audiences today are accustomed to being blasted by sound, so we must learn to live with them and use them properly. Warn your singers not to get too close or in the chorus songs they will be in competition with themselves, good modern microphones are very sensitive and if your audience is overwhelmed by amplified sound they just won't sing. Don't allow your Chairman to make any reference to microphones—it only draws attention to their anachronistic presence.

**Scenery**

The short answer to the problem of scenery is to have none at all —a few flowers and some tastefully arranged drapes and swags are all you require: you don't even need house-tabs. But if you have the facilities, money and man-power to be more adventurous with stage-dressings the first thing I would suggest is to install red plush velvet runners on a tab-track (both of which can be hired quite inexpensively) about five feet above the footlights. Of course many theatres will have a tab-track *in situ* which halves the difficulty. But do go for red plush—it looks so opulent.

Then, as a framework for the runners, construct a false proscenium consisting of a border above and trementors on either side decorated with scrolls and tassels, cherubs and Cupids in lush pinks and sinfully decadent golds and crimsons.

The trementors should be well angled on stage (more red plush for masking!) to make a very attractive and cosy setting for the front-cloth acts. For the intervals your scenic designer could perhaps provide a cloth displaying cod advertisements such as "Blogg's Finest old Gin—2d. a Quart!" Local firms and stores might co-operate on supplying copy for a cloth of this type and help to share the cost. It will be hung on the lines immediately above the front runners, and will also be on display as the audience enters the auditorium before the show; as the overture starts the runners will close and the cloth can then be flown out. It can also be used for the patter act or any front-cloth comedy routines.

If you have no flies (or even if you have) and your stage-management can cope with the technicalities a "roller" cloth makes a beautiful period effect.

Half-way down the acting area you will want another set of runners in a neutral gold or fawn. These can be varied to suit the mood required by changing the gellies in the flood-lights in the wings, and by adjusting the angular relationship between the drapes and the floods: if the angle is broad the drapes will be blandly lit, if acute the folds will be highlighted—especially useful for the operatic spot. At the rear of the stage will be a final set of runners or static tabs, or perhaps a cyclorama in front of which can be placed your settings.

These will only be tokens, since there are far too many items of short duration in a Music Hall for more elaboration to be necessary or desirable. A couple of free-standing returns, a trellis interweaved with paper flowers, a French flat—three simple settings are quite sufficient for the purpose—with perhaps one or two full cloths for the scenas.

Production Guide                                                15

## Useful Publications

The magazine *Contacts* which is issued twice yearly by The Spotlight Ltd, of 42 Cranbourn Street, London WC2H 7AP, contains many addresses of costume and property hire firms, scene builders and painters, removal firms, agencies, managements, theatre organizations and much other information of use primarily to the professional. An even more comprehensive list of managements and firms supplying all theatrical requirements is given in the *British Theatre Directory*, Richmond House, 12/13 Richmond Buildings, Dean Street, London W1V 5AF.

CHAPTER TWO
# THE PROGRAMME PROPER

## Cross-Overs

I feel that cross-overs are more suited to Revue than to Music Hall and avoid them in my own productions. Performers generally seem to enjoy them far more than audiences, and although I recognize how useful they can be in giving under-used members of your company something to do they encourage self-indulgence.

## Barber-Shop Quartets

These are always enormously popular, and I invariably include one in my own shows. If I haven't four men available, I alter the business and harmonies and perform the routine with three men—one of whom can be the Chairman. The performers don't have to be dressed as barbers; tail suits are just as effective, and save you a few pounds on costume hire since the evening-dress will probably come in handy elsewhere in your programme.

But however hysterically funny the act is, it is important for the harmonies to be sung well—the act will be all the more appreciated if it is musically attractive as well as humorous. There are many songs which lend themselves to barber-shop treatment: "*Wait Till The Clouds Roll By*", "*Silver Threads Among The Gold*", "*White Wings*", and "*Comrades*", which has a final *agitato* verse that might have been written for comedy performance. (These are published by E.M.I., except for "*Silver Threads*" which is Paxton's).

A quartet treatment of "*Wait Till The Clouds Roll By*" is given in my *Make 'Em Roar* Volume Two.

## Duets

Romantic duets provide a very satisfactory interlude in a programme, and can easily be concocted by slight adjustments to the lyrics of such numbers as "*While Strolling Through The

*Park*" or "*Little Annie Roonie*" (E.M.I.). Again, comedy duets can be built round such old favourites as "*Excelsior!*" (Boosey & Hawkes) or "*Tell Me Pretty Maiden*" (E.M.I.).

"Straight" duettists, like speciality performers, are often reluctant to change their acts to conform to the Music Hall style; in which case I can only say that you must be firm, otherwise ten minutes of songs from *South Pacific* or *Oklahoma* will effectively dissipate any sense of period your production may have achieved.

Don't forget the possibility of duets for two men: "*The Buttercup Song*" (from Sullivan and Burnand's *Cox and Box*) and "*Tenor And Baritone*" (published by Reeder & Walsh) are two excellent examples, or for two women, "*Pipes Of Pan Are Calling*" (Chappell's) never fails to bring the house down.

### Sketches

Sometimes an entire "half" is given over to a melodrama. By all means include a sketch of this type in your programme, but unless you are very sure of the capabilities of your cast and a reasonable degree of sophistication in your likely audience, make it a short one. I have myself published a number of suitable sketches (see Preface to the 2nd Edition) which are simple to mount and are well-proven in performance.

I have also on occasion used mime-sketches; these can be worked up on such celebrated poems as "*Dangerous Dan McGrew*" (Reynold's), "*The Lighthouse-Keeper's Daughter*" (French's) and "*And The Great Big Saw Came Nearer And Nearer*" (E.M.I.), although this last is more a song than a poem which I work with one girl as the heroine and one man playing all the other parts by changing hats.

The only two general points I would mention concerning the playing of melodrama sketches are (a) the cast must deliver their lines out front, difficult as this may seem at first; and (b) they *must* be played in deadly earnest. If the audience becomes aware that the cast finds the plot and the situations as ridiculous as they do themselves the humour is lost and the whole enterprise becomes sterile. So no corpsing, please. . . .

### Mime

Mime can also be used for a solo item, but only if you have a specialist in the field in your own company. Discreet musical accompaniment should always be used, to avoid any semblance of preciousness. Each item within the act can either be introduced by the Chairman or by the mime by displaying a suitable placard. An act of this type should not last longer than five minutes at most, and be used as a novelty interlude.

### Recitations

I rarely use straight dramatic recitations in my own programmes, though I would not by any means rule them out. John Hollis's rendition of *"Billy's Rose"* by George R. Sims always elicits thunderous applause, but then he is an extremely fine and experienced actor. Arthur Calder-Marshall's edition of Sims poetry is published by Hutchinson under the title *"Prepare To Shed Them Now"*.

My own versions of *"The Pigtail of Fu Manchu"* by Sax Rohmer and W. S. Gilbert's macabre *"Yarn Of The Nancy Belle"* can be found in my *"Make 'Em Roar"* Volume One; in Volume Two is a two-handed version of *"The Green Eye Of The Little Yellow God"* which is simple to perform and extremely effective. These are broad comedy items but if you think your audience will appreciate the baroque style and you have an actor capable of undertaking them poor old William McGonagall's extraordinary poetic effusions, published by Gerald Duckworth, are sure to raise shrieks of mirth.

### Song Sources

Most Music Hall songs are published by E.M.I. of 138-140 Charing Cross Road, London WC2, who have taken over the Francis, Day and Hunter and Feldman lists. The old Lawrence Wright list is now published by ATV Music Ltd., 19 Upper Brook Street, London W1, and the Paxton list by Novello & Co, 3 Upper James Street, London W1. The Reynold's list is obtainable from Keith Prowse Music Co Ltd., at 138 Charing Cross Road, London WC2 and the Campbell Connelly list from Music Sales Ltd., 78 Newman Street, London W1. Other useful addresses (mainly for ballads) are Boosey & Hawkes of 295 Regent Street, London W1 and Chappell's (incorporating Ascherberg, Hopwood and Crew) who are at 50, New Bond Street, London W1. A newcomer is

International Music Publications, 60/70, Roden Street, Ilford, Essex, whose four collections entitled "*Music Hall*" each contain twenty useful songs culled from various lists.

Some of the publishing houses provide catalogues on application, but if you have difficulty finding a particular song and your local sheet-music shop cannot trace it, contact the Repertoire Service Department of the Performing Right Society at 29, Berners Street, London W1 (01-580 5544) which will give you the name, address and phone number of the current publisher. If the publisher no longer has the number in print or is unable to locate a file copy for photocopying you may strike lucky at Francis Music Supply, 12 Gerrard Street, London W1 (01-437 2532), failing which your only recourse is to go to the British Library in Bloomsbury, obtain a temporary Reader's ticket and copy the song out by hand or have it photocopied on the premises—this is a chore you will have to do personally as the Library will not research for you and items may not be taken out.

**Scenas**

The scena, or medley of songs in a production setting, can be based on any theme you care to think of—love, the seaside, London, and so on. Three I have used often are on Food and Drink, the First World War, and Transport. A pub setting is a good framework for practically any song and any gag (with the Chairman donning an apron to become the Landlord). If you are pushed for rehearsal time, the "Cavalcade of Choruses" is a handy standby—each number to follow *segue* and everybody on for "*After The Ball*" (E.M.I.).

The timing of a scena must be carefully controlled—in rehearsal I check each item with a stopwatch. Since the average verse lasts for about thirty seconds and the average chorus the same, a contribution of chorus-verse-chorus will last for $1\frac{1}{2}$ minutes. If you have six principals this will run you into 9 minutes before you've thought about what the rest of the company will be doing. Scenas can so easily get out of hand, so you must be firm with your cast; one chorus sung solo and repeated by *omnes* is often sufficient to further your chosen theme—I do not believe that a scena is the place to work a number fully with all the verses and choruses: save that for the solo turn.

Scenas have two problems: the artistes must have time to change before it starts and the numbers must be selected to give a

*Production Guide*

reasonable contrast of mood, subject and tempo. If your M.D. is on the ball he can organize two choruses to be sung simultaneously, or arrange a sequence of snippets of choruses to be sung *segue*, e.g. four bars of the *"Eton Boating Song"* can be inserted with great effect into the end of *"Row Row Row"* (E.M.I.). To make the idea clearer I give details of my Food and Drink scene. This runs for ten minutes approximately, and features a few linking lines of patter from the cast between some of the items (not given here):

| | |
|---|---|
| G1 *Ingénue*/Juvenile Comedienne | M1 Principal Comic |
| G2 Principal Girl Singer | M2 Character Man |
| G3 Character Lady | M3 Principal Male Singer/Chairman |
| V Verse | C Chorus |

After the Chairman's introduction, the stage is darkened and a follow-spot picks up G2 entering UR. She carries a cloth-covered basket.

| 1 *"Caller Herrin' "* | Slow 2/4 | | Once through G2 | 30″ |
|---|---|---|---|---|

During this song, accompanied by solo flute, the rest of the cast gradually wanders on stage in the half-light (except G3 who is changing, having performed the previous act). After *"Caller Herrin' "* there is a little back-chat, leading to:

| 2 *"Having A Bit Tonight"* | Fast 6/8 | CC | M1 | 45″ |
|---|---|---|---|---|
| Patter | | | | |
| 3 *"Picking All The Big Ones Out"* | Fast 2/4 | CVC | G1 | 45″ |
| Patter | | | | |
| 4 *"The Cucumber Song"* | Fast 2/4 | CVC Coda | M2 | 90″ |

Segue fortissimo of G3

| 5 *"The Marrow Song"* | Free V, C fast 6/8 | VCVC | G3 | 120″ |
|---|---|---|---|---|

Segue

| 6a *"Boiled Beef and Carrots"* | 4 bars of C only | | omnes | |
|---|---|---|---|---|
| b *"I Do Like An Egg For My Tea"* | Bouncy 3/4 | C | G1 | 15″ |

Segue

| 7 *"What I Want Is A Proper Cup Of Coffee"* | Steady 4/4 | C | M1 | 15″ |
|---|---|---|---|---|

Patter from Chairman

| 8 *"Beer Glorious Beer"* | Slow 3/4 | ½VC | M3 | 45″ |
|---|---|---|---|---|

Diminuendo on final note of chorus; the lights lower and trombone plays first four bars of *"Drinking"* solo with cast humming four-part harmony. Segue into:

9   "*Drink To Me Only*"         Slow 3/4                     G2       90″

Cast hum first 16 bars then sing the remaining 16 bars in harmony under the melody with solo flute accompaniment. Lights up for applause. Segue into:

10   "*Come Where The Booze Is Cheaper!*"     Steady 4/4    C         omnes    15″

Sung by cast in four-part harmony unaccompanied.

Segue

11   *Finale:* medley of some of the preceding songs, with words and tempi in a *mélange*

## Marching Routines

These require a great deal of rehearsal time but are well worth the trouble spent—provided your participants can drill properly: a burlesque is only funny when it is apparent that the performers know their business. A routine of this kind consists simply of three or more men executing a drill and march routine to a suitable medley of bouncy march tunes (i.e. in 2/4 time rather than 4/4); one of the three makes one mistake after the other reducing the other two to apoplexy and chaos. The best ending for this act is for the awkward squad to march off, the calls being further crossings of the stage from wing to wing with a different joke on each appearance.

Precision is essential, even in the "mistakes" (or perhaps especially in the "mistakes"), and the drill needs to be overseen by someone with military experience.

Suitable accompaniments might be a medley of Sousa marches —one tune should not be repeated *ad nauseam*—or a medley composed of the following: "*El Abanico*" by Javaloyes (Boosey & Hawkes), "*Women*" from Lehar's *Merry Widow* (Chappell's), and the two Lionel Monckton favourites "*Moonstruck*" from *Our Miss Gibbs* and "*Charming Weather*" from *The Arcadians* (both Chappell's).

## The Cast

It is very dispiriting to sit through an evening of rum-ti-tum ditties sung in home-spun "natural" voices, so try to ensure that you have at least one really good singer in your cast.

Then you will need one patter comic, an *ingénue*, a juvenile man, a character man and woman, plus assorted boys and girls

## Production Guide

for your sketches and scenas. And a Chairman, of course, but we have discussed him at length earlier, and in any case Part II of this Book is devoted to his interests, so he needs no more attention here.

How large should your cast be? This is sometimes decided for you by the nature of the company presenting the Music Hall. If it is for a Professional Repertory Company you will have to make do with the artistes already under contract—although I always insist on taking in one or two specialists in this field, since you cannot expect to find first-class singers and dancers in a company of straight actors. If you are producing for an amateur company, you will be expected to use any and all of the members who wish to take part. You will then have to consult the Committee (dread institution!) and hold auditions. And the best of luck.

I once found myself, when engaged to produce for an amateur company, obliged to use a lady whose talents had not impressed me at the auditions. But because she was responsible for the society getting their hall for free, I was instructed to use her in my show. I felt this was a bad start and put my foot down, with the result that someone else did the production.

I never use more than six people for my own shows, plus a Chairman. In fact if money is tight I dispense with one of the men and incorporate myself as Chairman into the sketch and barber-shop quartet.

With any cast, large or small, you need to contrast your types. If you have three principal girls, you will want them to be of differing heights, colouring and personalities. I once took a company on tour for seven months in which my *ingénue* was petite and blonde, my principal singer was tall and brunette, and my character lady was bonny and auburn! But one isn't always so lucky. The men should similarly complement each other, and should couple up well with the ladies, if you'll pardon the expression. Your principal lady singer will not thank you for having to sing duets with a boy three inches shorter, nor will your character lady be best pleased at being partnered in a scena with a lad young enough to be her son.

And your cast should feature exponents of all the requisite talents: there must be, as I have said, one good patter comic, one *really* good singer, one featured dancer, one "big personality", and so on, so that the corporate effect will be one of a company of multiple talents and panache.

The intimate revue-style of production, with everyone changing costumes and make-ups like crazy and demonstrating stunning versatility, will be very hard work for your cast, but the warmth of affection and contact they will build up through the evening will more than compensate for any sweat lost.

A large cast should be split into principals and chorus. If this causes any pain you might explain that this is quite the established practice with a Musical Play or a Savoy Opera, and that there is no other way of handling the problem. If your audience sees a constant stream of new faces, each appearing for no more than a few minutes at a time, there will be no chance to establish any personal rapport and the intimacy which is so much part of a Music Hall will never be attained. To illustrate the point, some years ago I was visiting Las Vegas, and naturally went to see as many of the big spectacular shows for which the city is famous as I could. One of these featured two of the most elaborate scenes I have ever seen in my life. On the gigantic stage were colossal sets, huge staircases receding way up into the flies, and an immaculately dressed cast of over a hundred. The applause which greeted the close of these scenes scarcely lasted long enough to bring the tabs in, whereas the single acts were very well received. The moral? Scenery and anonymous hordes of chorus leave an audience cold; what really appeals is a strong individual personality. So forget the revolving stage, the ship-sinking-in-full-sight, the "real" horse-race, and Storming of the Bastille—just make sure your principals can "get across", and if you find you have one enormous burning talent on your hands, it is your responsibility to give it every chance to blaze.

**The Comic**

As producer, you have the right and the duty to hear a comic's patter before the show opens, if only to ensure that there is no repetition of gags, which is a contretemps I have seen happen more than once. But so often a comic will say to you: ". . . oh, I haven't worked out all my material yet," or he will plead that he "can't do it without an audience . . .". You must be firm, and insist that he runs through his gags, even if he mutters them to you in a dark corner somewhere.

Comics are notoriously apt to overrun their time if the act is going well. There isn't much you can do about this while the

*Production Guide* 25

show is actually in progress, but if you impress upon him in rehearsals the importance of not taking up more than his allotted time, you may be able to bring him to heel.

It is customary for comics to finish with a song. Try to keep this down to a couple of choruses, or at most a chorus, verse and final chorus, or the act will double in length. It is also customary for the Chairman to be the target for some ruderies from the comic. I am all for this, but it should not be prolonged for two reasons: the audience will always instinctively look at the person who is the butt of a gag, thus distracting from the comic himself. And, if the remarks are too outrageous they will totally lose credibility and thus be diminished in effect. It is better for the comic to throw a couple of cracks at the Chair, and then talk about a mythical friend or brother whose eccentricities the audience can accept because they can't see him.

How long his act should run is entirely at your discretion. It depends on how good he is and what is the content of the rest of the show. If you are short on comedy and there is not much talking in the rest of the show—if, for instance, there is no recitation and your sketch is short—then you may give him as much as ten or twelve minutes, *including* his closing number. But generally speaking I would limit him to eight minutes, including the song. If he complains, tell him that he will make himself unpopular with his fellow artistes if he hogs too large a share of the available time, that he should leave his audience wanting more, that eight minutes is quite long enough for a patter act, that *of course* he can do himself justice in such a short time because he is such a funny fellow—tell him anything you like, but don't let him go on and on until he kills himself stone dead—another misfortune I have witnessed sadly on more occasions than I care to remember.

Watch his material, too. He must on no account mention television, jet-planes or Raquel Welch—gramophones, the Wright Brothers ("they've gone wrong again!") and Lillie Langtry must be substituted, and if this spoils the gag, then cut it entirely.

Nor must he be allowed to become too crude—smut and vulgarity are perfectly acceptable (indeed expected) providing it is *period* smut and vulgarity. Jokes about dirty old men and fruity housewives are O.K., jokes about the Pill and homosexuality are not. So often I have seen an audience switch right off when a comic gets too blue—once, I am sorry to say, in a production of my own.

Whether your comic's material is likely to go beyond acceptable bounds is a matter solely for your own judgement. The type of audience you are likely to get (senior citizens especially resent being subjected to blue material) is one factor to be taken into consideration, further than which I cannot advise except to say that this is a danger to watch out for.

**Style and Presentation**

How difficult it is to talk about style for a Music Hall! The Chairman is mainly responsible for setting the standard in this respect, but your soloists must also consider their performances seriously in a Victorian/Edwardian ambiance.

One simple but very effective instruction you can give is that all your artistes (except in the sketch and the scenas) should acknowledge the Chairman at the beginning and end of their respective appearances. After a suitably laudatory introduction for, say, your operatic soprano, she can be discovered on as the runners open and incline her head graciously to the Chairman, as though approving the truth and beauty of his remarks. Entering after a perhaps less than fulsome introduction, your comic can tip his hat to the Chairman with a wry grin.

All artistes addressing the audience will not just say, "... ladies and gentlemen", but will say, "... Mr Chairman, ladies and gentlemen". At the conclusion of each act the artiste will bow or curtsy to the audience, extend a hand to the band and finally again acknowledge the Chairman. The point of all this fal-la is to help establish and maintain the polite fiction that the Chairman is an extremely important person and is in charge of the proceedings. Besides, it looks nice.

Don't allow your Chairman to inform the audience in his opening patter that the show will "take them back . . .". The object of all your careful advertising and dressing of the foyer and auditorium is that the audience will *already* be "back", and to draw attention to the reverse is to destroy that illusion right at the start.

It goes without saying that your show will not include any modern numbers, but I do not insist that none of the songs you use should have been published later than, say, 1918. If a song sounds

## Production Guide

right, then by all means use it. *Don't Dilly Dally* (Feldman's), for instance, dates from as late as 1919! Three numbers I have often used are "*I'm Going Back To Himazas*" which I alter to "*We're Going Back, etc.*" and use as a rousing three-hander, "*The Marrow Song*" and "*Let's All Go To The Music Hall*" which is a superb company opener (All Lawrence Wright). The first is of twenties vintage and the other two from the thirties, but all three songs could have been written earlier; only a specialist will know and only a pedant will care.

Your artistes should present themselves as strongly delineated types: the saucy skivvy, the winsome young maiden, the cheeky coster, the stolid policeman, the upstanding young man-about-town, the toff, the blowzy harridan, etc. etc. Subtleties are out of place where characterization is concerned, although the technique of performance can be as subtle as the artiste can make it.

Movements should all be studied and choreographed, with the girls tripping balletically about the stage (watch the way girls in the circus leave the ring) and the men moving cleanly from position to position, from pose to pose, from attitude to attitude. Amateurs, alas, rarely seem to know the meaning of the word *repose*. They seem to think that all that is required of a Music Hall song is to flail their arms around and to jig about incessantly as though suffering from a particularly bad attack of St Vitus' Dance. Some artistes are like elephants in this respect—they never stand still.

Examine the verse of a number to see what it might yield and how it should best be illustrated, whether with the face, the hands, the legs, the body, use of a prop, or a combination of all the artiste's equipment. If the song is to consist of two verses and three choruses, study how the presentation can be arranged into a pattern, giving a balance and a symmetry to the whole. Your choreographer will help here.

First the artiste enters and acknowledges the Chairman. Or is he discovered on? What props and furniture are to be used, if any? What should the lighting be? What should the costume be? Is he on the full stage or only half-stage? Will he sing his number straight or comic—some numbers admit of either interpretation? Will he work it as a sober Englishman, a drunk Irishman or a canny Scotsman? It's a bit late to ask these questions now, for he is already on stage, but these are the kind of questions which should be asked when forming the framework for an act.

The first verse is being sung free, shall we say—it could be sung in tempo, but it is a bit of a mouthful and his diction isn't too good. For the first chorus, he sings in the same D.C. position without frills, business or elaboration; this is a good tune but isn't all that well known so we must give the audience a chance to learn it. Between the first chorus and the second verse the band plays eight bars, to enable the soloist to perform a little dance around— he can't really dance, but his movements are clean and neat, so we want to take advantage of this facet of his talents.

He finishes his dance D.L. and delivers the second verse, again freely, from there, walking to C. to make a point half-way through, and finishing by walking across to the Chairman to make another point to him. The Chairman smiles, the house-lights come up and the second chorus starts. The audience sings heartily, and laughs at the performer's eccentric dance or hand movements or production of a comic prop. At the end of the second chorus, the band plays a two-bar key-change lift and the audience roars out the third and final chorus, with the soloist happily strolling about the stage in a pre-arranged routine. The final note sees him D.C. again, with his prop in his hand, his hat in the other and a big smile on his face.

Notice that between the second and third choruses our man did not shout, "All together now!" and stand there conducting the audience haphazardly. He doesn't do this because he is not the Man in the White Suit at the Cup Final—he is a stage performer whose purpose is to entertain. The late Randolph Sutton never *demanded* that his audiences sing "*On Mother Kelly's Doorstep*" (E.M.I.); he gently indicated that he would be greatly obliged if we *cared* to join him—it was entirely up to us—and such was his charm that of course we did sing, because we wanted to please him. He would stand stock still for a few seconds, and then a smile would lighten his delicate face as he heard us start—he was so delighted that we had accepted his invitation—and then he would dance for us. He did not cease to entertain while we sang for him; he offered a *quid pro quo*, and everyone was satisfied.

For the third and/or final chorus the artiste will have something in reserve—a descant line over the melody or a fresh turn in the choreography, or a sight gag perhaps, e.g. in "*There Was I Waiting At The Church*" (E.M.I.) on the line "... he sent me round a note ...", the unfortunate young virgin can fish around for the note,

# Production Guide 29

flourish it and hurl it away. On each successive chorus a new note is produced from a different part of her apparel, and for the final chorus she will naturally turn up stage, lift up her dress and take it from her knickers. She will then take it over to the Chairman for him to verify the truth of its contents; he will take it very gingerly indeed between the tips of his thumb and forefinger, glance at it hurriedly and distastefully hand it back with an expression of fastidious distaste. This will be too much for the poor girl—even the Chairman, normally the very soul of courtesy, has rejected her, and off she goes in floods of tears. Even the applause from the audience fails to cheer her up when she reappears to take her call; she casts one final despairing look at the Chairman whose watch has unaccountably stopped and is engaging all his attention and then makes her final dejected exit.

As indicated in this example, when the audience is roaring out a chorus, the artiste may stop singing and indulge in some suitable byplay—Hetty King's pipe business during the final chorus of *"All The Nice Girls Love A Sailor"* is legendary.

Finally, I would deem it a personal favour if you can stop your artistes ordering their audience to clap in time with the music. It seems to be mandatory in club entertainment that we have to exhaust ourselves slapping our palms together. "Come on, now ..." shouts the "all-round entertainer", sweating with desperation. "Let's have a party!" I resent this peremptory instruction—apart from anything else, it hurts. We always get out of time after eight bars anyway, fail to stop for the performer's "Big finish" and so are left to fade out disconsolately. If the beat is strong enough and the number is swinging along, I will clap with the best will in the world. But if I am commanded to do so, my enthusiasm drains away faster than bathwater down the plughole.

## Constructing the Programme

I have listed at the start of the previous chapter some of the items which may be included in your programme. In my own productions I try to include as much as is representative of the Music Hall format—so, apart from the solo turns, I would advise you to include one sketch, two scenas (one to open and one to close), one patter act, one or two duets, one song-and-dance and one operatic spot. This list is by no means comprehensive, of course: there are also male impersonations, Dame acts, black-face, mime acts, instrumental turns, and speciality acts such as conjuring or juggling. And there is the "Tribute To . . ." routine, which is a thin excuse to string together half a dozen Marie Lloyd or Albert Chevalier numbers, and the recitation—one very good comedy/pathos monologue is "*I Ain't 'Arf A Lucky Kid*" (Reynold's) to be performed by your *ingénue* which might make a pleasing novelty. Other suggestions are the comedy cod strong man act, and the obviously phoney mind-reading act—"What am I touching now? *Watch* what you are saying . . . !" "A watch!" "Correct!" This routine is given in full in my "*Make 'Em Roar*" Volume Two.

So, let us settle down with pencil and paper and consider what we might offer. Ten minutes before curtain time, we have the floats brought up to full, to present a cheerful prospect to our incoming audience. We then start, straightforwardly enough, with the overture, the Chairman's entrance, opening patter and chorus song—this needs to be a very well-known song indeed to help the audience ease themselves into letting their hair down. "*Daisy Belle*" (E.M.I.) is very suitable for this—I have used it even in America—being both familiar and *easy to sing*.

We start, again straightforwardly, with something rousing: a scena perhaps or a snappy three-handed routine. I have already mentioned "*Himazas*"; another favourite of mine for this spot is "*Beside The Seaside*" (Francis, Day and Hunter) which, if you wish, can lead into a scena of seaside songs.

Or (and this is especially useful if the dressing-rooms are only approachable from the auditorium) you can get everyone on with "*Down At The Old Bull And Bush*" (Feldman's) with your cast wandering through the tables and chairs out front. They all arrive on stage at the end of the chorus and *segue* into, say, "*Knocked 'Em In The Old Kent Road*" (Reynold's) which in turn leads very happily into "*Knees Up Mother Brown*". A black-out and *Exeunt Omnes*, and there you have your nice bright opening and your cast in the wings where their changes of costume have been pre-set.

If you have the luxury of dressing-rooms backstage, this problem will not arise, in which case may I advise that whatever you do open with and however your programme runs, you try to save one artiste for much later on in the programme. A fresh face half-

## Production Guide

way through the evening is such a pleasant surprise for an audience.

You will be closing the programme with some kind of scena or concerted item which you will precede with a strong comedy item. Prior to that perhaps will be your comedy barber-shop quartet (at that time of night you don't have to worry too much about following one comedy item with another), and, to revert to the first half, you will follow the opening scena with a quiet gentle number performed by a solo girl.

Our problem now is to fill in the substantial gap which remains between the start and the close. Whatever you decide should present a gradually rising graph-line. At times the line may run horizontally as the show changes gear and the audience catches its wind, but the line must never be allowed to dip down. After the "horizontal line" of the solo girl (and none the worse for that), the programme will need a sharp lift which is why I suggest that you now bring on your patter comic. He will scream and rage and rend his garments at being given such a *terrible* spot, but I can only say with all the sincerity at my command that this is a very good place indeed for a patter act—my partner, Johnny Dennis, and I have for many years performed our own double patter acts at this point in the programme and have never seen fit to change the placing. You can explain to your broken-hearted clown that this position in the programme also helps to establish his comic genius for later hilarious appearances.

Besides, the show will now have been running for about twenty minutes, and the audience will *need* some patter. While we're on the subject, another good place for a patter act is, believe it or not, immediately after the interval when the audience has just had a drink and sung the entr'acte chorus.

For a season I was resident Chairman at a Music Hall in Croydon and due to a shortage of acts had to do a solo spot in every programme. Since there was rarely a patter comic on the bill I used to supply the deficiency with ten minutes of gags myself, and immediately after the interval was the place that I chose—not third spot in the first half as suggested above, however, because as Chairman I had only just opened the show and felt therefore that it was too soon to inflict myself upon the audience again.

Another little wrinkle for your comic: if he is doing two solo spots he should use his strongest material *first*. Chaplin was celebrated for this technique in his silent films—the best gags came early to soften the audience up, after which they would laugh at anything. A very experienced and tremendously powerful comedienne, Pamela Cundell, who I am proud to say has appeared in many of my own Music Halls, once gave me the same explanation when I asked her why she wanted to do the stronger of her two acts first. "Always do your best material on your first entrance," she replied, and of course she was right.

So if your comic wants to save himself until just prior to the finale, talk him out of it. By that time your audience will be a little jaded with all the splendours you have unfolded before their eyes, they will have begun to tire and a patter comic is especially vulnerable before a sated, weary and possibly over-warm audience. No, get him on for the third spot in the first half while the house is fresh and looking forward to the goodies you have in store. Remember the graph-line—its upward curve will have begun to flatten out by the last half-hour, and you don't want a catastrophic dip just before the close.

After the interval, presuming there is only one, you will want to place, for instance, a three-handed version of "*Here We Are Again*" (E.M.I.) or a comedy two-handed version with patter of "*I Live In Trafalgar Square*" after which might follow your straight operatic spot consisting of all the old favourites—"*Vilia*" (Chappell's), "*My Hero*", "*Smilin' Through*" (both E.M.I.), "*The Sunshine Of Your Smile*" (E.M.I.), "*Love's Old Sweet Song*" (Boosey & Hawkes), are the sort of thing your audience will adore. They won't want anything too difficult, so grand opera excerpts should be limited "*The Laughing Song*", "*One Fine Day*", "*On With The Motley*", "*Voi Che Sapete*" and other well-established favourites. Your baritone must sing "*The Floral Dance*" (Chappell's) and your bass must, of course, sing "*The Lost Chord*" (Boosey & Hawkes).

All this may sound at best corny and at worst patronizing. I concede the former and am not ashamed of it, but the latter I would dispute: in a Music Hall we are not trying to educate, we are attempting to entertain, and these old songs have not lasted without good reason—they remain damn fine songs which when well sung still retain the power to make an audience yell for more. The opera spot, therefore, should be perhaps the longest solo item: two numbers and a prepared encore, to last from 8 to

*Production Guide*

10 minutes. This will possibly be the first appearance by the singer, and so will have a suitably reverential (but not cod) introduction by the Chairman. After an hour or more of bawling out jolly little ditties the audience will be in the mood to relax and hear a sweet undemanding aria or two, and the performer will be pleasantly surprised by the warmth of the reception.

How is our programme shaping up? This is how it looks so far:

*Min*
- $1\frac{1}{2}$ Overture
- $4\frac{1}{2}$ Chairman's Opening Patter and first Chorus Song
- 10 Opening Scene
- 5 Solo Girl—"*I Was A Good Little Girl Till I Met You*" or "*Ain't It Nice?*" (Both E.M.I.)
- 8 Patter

29

- 15 Interval

- $\frac{1}{2}$ Entr'acte
- 2 Chairman. Loyal Toast
- 5 Opening routine
- 9 Opera Spot

- 6 Barber-Shop Quartet
- 9 Strong Comedy Spot
- 10 Closing Scene
- $1\frac{1}{2}$ Chairman's Farewell and Exit Chorus

43
**Total** 87 minutes

So thus far we have planned a total of 87 minutes out of our total of approximately 135, leaving us 48 to fill. Since the first half has only 29 minutes and we want this to run longer than the second half we need to add about another 36 minutes, leaving us with 12 minutes to add to the second half, giving:

$$\begin{aligned} \text{First half: } 29 + 36 &= 65 \\ \text{Second half: } 43 + 12 &= 55 \\ \text{Interval: } &\phantom{=}\ 15 \\ \hline &\phantom{=}135 \end{aligned}$$

Each solo act, with the Chairman's intro., performance and calls, can usually be timed at 5 minutes, but since in my experience shows always run longer than anticipated the 12 remaining minutes for the second half can be taken for only two more acts. The opera spot—notoriously difficult to follow—might be succeeded by the recitation, which can be either cod or straight. If it is straight the show will be in danger of taking itself too seriously and so must be followed by a boisterous chorus number. If cod, it can still be followed by a rousing song with a good beaty chorus, since the audience will not have sung for some time and will be ready for the chance to let off steam.

But what do we close the first half with? This spot can be quite successfully taken by the sketch—especially if it is one which leaves props strewn all over the stage and your cast pinned and strapped into costumes which will take the interval to get out of.

Alternatively, if the sketch needs props and furniture to be pre-set, you can place it second in the second half, with the opening routine of the second half taking place on the apron in front of the runners. The first half can then be closed by the opera spot—if your singer is especially sensational, I would recommend this course of action in any case, since opera spots can so often overwhelm an audience and leave them inattentive for what follows.

(If you decide to put the sketch in the second half, omit the recitation in the third spot or your timing will go all awry, and in any case you don't want two "talking" items together. The recitation can be sandwiched between two musical items in the first half instead—preferably towards the end.)

The opera spot, if it does close the first half, may be preceded by a strong comedy concerted item—perhaps a routine with a girl and an idiot chorus of boys: "*If I Should Plant A Tiny Seed Of Love*" (E.M.I.) or vice versa in "*A Bachelor Gay Am I*" (E.M.I.) with one of the "girls" being the comic in drag.

But whatever you close the first half with, remember the adage: "Send 'em happy to the bars...."

Now the show is looking like this:

*Min.*
1½ Overture
4½ Chairman's Welcome. First Chorus Song
10 Opening Scena

## Production Guide

     5  Solo girl
     8  Patter
    10  Sketch *or* Opera Spot
    —
39

15  Interval
     ½  Entr'acte
     2  Chairman's Welcome back. Loyal Toast
     5  Opener—two- or three-hander
    10  Opera Spot *or* Sketch
     5  Recitation. (omit if the Sketch precedes) *or* Speciality
     5  Rousing Chorus song
     6  Barber-Shop quartet
    10  Final Comedy Solo
    10  Closing Scena
    1½  Chairman's Farewell and Final Chorus
    —
55
**Total** 109 minutes

Now we have our 55 minute second half (of course, some acts may be longer or shorter than suggested here. The Chairman's "Welcome Back" may be protracted if there are Birthday or Wedding Anniversaries to be acknowledged—but this example gives an idea of the planning procedure) and we have filled in 39 minutes of the first half into which we must now insert 26 minutes or approximately five acts. We have had no duet yet, and some of the cast will still be without a solo appearance.

With regard to the equitable sharing-out of stage time among your artistes, I find it a help to nominate them all as indicated in the scena breakdown on page 19; this ensures that you do not find yourself giving all the plums to G1 or M2, besides ensuring that everyone has time to change.

You would do well to follow the patter act in the first half with a solo. This can be for either boy or girl, whichever suits the programme the better and whatever talents you may have at your disposal. This in turn can be followed by a duet, and then another solo—perhaps a soft-shoe dance. It may be that if your sketch is placed after this dance spot and is longer than 10 minutes I have allotted you will now have 65 minutes and the first half will be complete. But if the sketch is to be in the second half and you intend to close the first with the operatic spot, you will need to precede it with a strong comedy turn—perhaps the barber-shop quartet which will not now be needed in the second half for reasons of time. And you can slide in the recitation between the duet and the dance spot, or omit it altogether.

So, the final running-order will look something like this:

**Min.**
- 1½ Overture
- 4½ Chairman's Patter
- 10 Opening Scena
- 5 Solo Girl
- 8 Patter
- 5 Solo—girl or boy with Chorus Song
- 5 Duet
- 5 Recitation (?) or Novelty Comedy item
- 5 Solo—boy or girl with dance
- 6 Concerted item or Barber-Shop Quartet
- 10 Sketch or Opera Spot

65

- 15 Interval

- ½ Entr'acte
- 2 Chairman. Loyal Toast
- 5 Opener
- 10 Opera Spot or Sketch
- 5 Recitation or Chorus song if after Sketch. Or Omit. Or Speciality
- 5 Rousing Chorus song
- 6 Barber-Shop Quartet or Concerted item
- 10 Final Comedy Solo Spot
- 10 Closing Scena
- 1½ Chairman's Farewell and Final Chorus

55

Total 135

I don't feel it matters if two men follow each other with solo items, provided they are well contrasted; but I always avoid putting two ladies next to one another. Anyone without a solo spot and not featured well in the sketch can perhaps be mollified by being given plenty to do in the scenas. But whatever running-order you do come up with, you can be sure that someone will feel hard done by. However, that is life, and the part must be subordinated to the whole. If you feel your whole programme is going to be thrown out of kilter because of an objection by someone who feels himself slighted, resist the temptation to "avoid trouble" and stick to your principles. As a last resort, refer him to me—I once sacked a man half-way across the Pacific Ocean and sent him home from Los Angeles, so when I say be firm, I mean—*be firm*. ...

You may find yourself having to adjudicate between two artistes vying for the same number. "But you *promised* that I could do it...." "I've been doing this number since before you were born...." And so on and so on. This is the sort of thing you may have to cope with, which is why I always indulge in an orgy of careful pre-production planning and telephoning before rehearsals start.

You may also find to your dismay that you have on your hands two comic parsons, three comic charladies, four Chelsea Pensioners and an unlimited number of horrid little pubescent schoolgirls; so when you ask your artistes which numbers they would care to perform, make sure you also know how the number is to be worked. Many numbers can be performed in an infinite variety of ways, and you don't want to adjudicate between clashes of this sort if you can avoid it. When all else fails—as with deciding which comedian shall use a certain gag—the cowardly way out is to spin a coin in the presence of the disputants.

Then, again, you may have a scena nicely worked out and you will say to your nice-looking juvenile male: "What I want here, Aubrey, is something softly sentimental in 3/4 time. Have you got anything suitable?" And young Aubrey will answer and say, "Well ... I do a super version of *'I'm 'Enery The Eighth I Am'*. Can't you fit that in?" Your reply *must* be, "I'm afraid not, Aubrey. Next time, perhaps. Meanwhile, here's *'Sweet Rosie O'Grady'*—have a think about one verse and two choruses by tomorrow, will you, there's a good chap? ... Elsie! Can I have a quick word ... ?" And you are away, before young Aubrey has time to stamp his foot.

On a slightly different tack, I was once promised the funniest cod dramatic recitation of all time, only to discover about a week from production that it was the full tear-jerking tragedy reading —"The Death Of Little Nell" from Dickens' *Old Curiosity Shop*, no less. That made my running-order look a bit sick, I can tell you, so as the tragedian wouldn't change his act he had to go.

As I have said earlier, if the stage equipment permits, you should vary your vistas. Patter acts and some quiet solo songs are suitable for performance on the apron ("*Ain't It Nice?*" is very sweet when sung by a pretty girl sitting on a stool D.C. in the follow-spot only); other acts such as your duet can take the half-stage, leaving the full stage for the scenas, the sketch and the major dance routines.

And just in case you need it, here is a suggested running-order for a show with two intervals. Note that the sketch does not figure in the third "half", which is far too late for an audience to concentrate on plot and dialogue. If the whole of the second half is taken up by the sketch, the first and third halves can stay as suggested below with the exception of the opening number of the first half which might in this instance be elaborated into a full scena:

|     | *Min.* |                                            |
|-----|--------|--------------------------------------------|
|     | 1½     | Overture                                   |
|     | 4½     | Chairman's Welcoming Patter                |
|     | 5      | Opening Concerted Item                     |
|     | 5      | Solo girl or boy. Gentle chorus number     |
|     | 8      | Patter                                     |
|     | 5      | Solo *or* double straight chorus number    |
|     | 6      | Strong comedy. Dame Spot *or* Barber-Shop Quartet |
| 35  |        |                                            |
| 10  |        | Interval                                   |
|     | ½      | Entr'acte                                  |
|     | 2      | Chairman. Loyal Toast                      |
|     | 10½    | London Scena                               |
|     | 6      | Comic vicar *or* Speciality act            |
|     | 5      | Song-sheet Chorus. With dance?             |
|     | 6      | Comedy Duet. Or omit if the sketch is long |
|     | 10     | Sketch                                     |
| 40  |        |                                            |
| 10  |        | Interval                                   |
|     | ½      | Entr'acte                                  |

|     |                                              |
| --- | -------------------------------------------- |
| 1   | Chairman                                     |
| 5   | Comedy duet *or* Patter *or* Concerted Item  |
| 10  | Opera Spot                                   |
| 5   | Recitation                                   |
| 5   | Rousing Chorus song. Boy or girl             |
| 5   | Barber-Shop Quartet *or* Strong Comedy Solo  |
| 7   | Final Scena                                  |
| 1½  | Chairman's Close and Farewell Exit           |

40

Total 135

## Alternatives

All right, so you hate my running-orders: what else is there in the Music Hall tradition? There is the full-length melodrama, with songs and dances inserted during the action for the principals to show their versatility, and with performances of traditional Music Hall turns on the apron during scene changes. This form of entertainment has a perfectly respectable pedigree and I have nothing at all against it; it is simply a different animal from the one we have been discussing.

Then there is the "Old Time Variety Show" which is generally nothing of the sort. This usually consists of half a dozen or so variety acts put into a Music Hall setting with few if any concessions to a period style. The Chairman will very likely be a superannuated Butlin's redcoat (*pace* Des O'Connor) who seems rather uncomfortable and out of his depth. The main difference between the form of this kind of show and the one I have been advocating is that the acts will be a good deal longer; they will be full acts in the professional meaning of the term, lasting for 15 or 20 minutes or so.

I don't care for this type of Music Hall myself, since despite its name it doesn't allow for sufficient variety and entirely lacks the ensemble spirit which in my earnest opinion is the *sine qua non* of Music Hall. And having used two Latin expressions in two paragraphs, I feel it is time that we reached the

## Coda

I am well aware that you may have read thus far with scorn and derision mounting in your breast. "But *we* didn't do that, and we had a tremendous success . . . !" is the sort of remark I imagine to be leaping to your lips. Or perhaps, "Surely *that's* obvious. What does he think I am—a half-wit?" Or even, "He doesn't say a *word* about So-and-so!"

To all of which I can only say: "I know." With regard to the "tremendous success" achieved in the teeth of my strictures, I will admit that there is more than one way to kill a cat. My good friend Norman Warwick performs superbly as a completely unorthodox Chairman—he wears a battered bowler and displays naked red braces over his collarless shirt; his Chairman is the very antithesis of the one I have described in these pages, and marvellous he is too. But then Norman has been performing in professional Music Hall (and musicals and plays not to mention The National Theatre) for many, many years, and knows how to break the rules. Walk before you can run, kiddies.

As to the obviousness of a point I may have raised: it may be obvious to *you*, sir, but spare a thought for the poor soul who has never even seen a Music Hall, let alone produced one, and pity his ignorance.

Overleaf begins the *raison d'être* of this book: the Chairman's patter. These preluding chapters have been added to provide what I hope may be taken as guidance for Music Hall production; if you find they help you, I shall be very pleased. If you find them confusing ramblings—just tear them out and forget them. I shan't mind.

*Part 2*

YOUR DISTINGUISHED CHAIRMAN

# THE ROLE OF THE CHAIRMAN

The role of the Chairman can be seen superficially as merely the man who introduces the acts; he is rather more than that, however, since he also sets the style, the tone and the character of the evening.

He should have "good address", as the Victorians themselves put it; he should have authority, charm, a good speaking voice (by which I don't mean an Oxford accent), a fluency of delivery and an ease of manner—in a word, though it's not a word I much like, he should be genial.

An actor friend of mine once said to me, "I saw you in the Chair at the Players' the other night. Do you know what I like about you as Chairman? You're so safe . . . one feels sure that no matter what happens or is said you will be able to handle it." I felt that this was the finest compliment I had ever been paid, especially since in that particular Music Hall the geography of the auditorium and the extreme sophistication of the regular patrons make every performance an ordeal.

Perhaps, then, this is one other quality that a Chairman needs —calmness. Perhaps it's the ability to persuade an audience to relax and to feel that all's for the best in the best of all possible worlds, even if the world he is creating and inviting them to enter is a fantasy world which alas doesn't exist outside the walls of Disneyland. The house must be swept up by the power of the Chairman's imagination and rhetoric into a never-never land of gaslight and phaetons, cheeky costers and saucy but virtuous maidens. A colourful, ingenuous world, where black and white are clearly delineated, attitudes are predictable and uncomplicated, and everything comes right in the end.

On the technical level, the role of the Chairman might best be approached as an actor tackles a farce, in that he knows the whole thing is absurd but must play it with all the earnestness and conviction at his command. The audience knows that the enterprise is fundamentally illusory, but they go along with the pretence because we would all like to think that the "good old days" just *might* have been like that.

This is why the cardinal sin the Chairman can commit is to dissipate the simulation of a Victorian or Edwardian entertainment by making anachronistic jokes. I once upset a comic considerably (in fact he pulled out of the show) by asking him to cut his references to television and the current Prime Minister; I could not make him understand that an audience will willingly meet a Chairman's assumption of their complicity in the game of make-believe, and so suddenly to dump them back in the dreary world of present-day reality is to break faith and to lose their confidence. And what a cruel thing to do to a good-natured, trusting audience, pathetically hoping to enjoy themselves by getting away from it all . . . they feel embarrassed; they've been had—they're not in the Naughty Nineties, after all.

In short, the current version of Old Time Music Hall is pure escapism, and the Chairman is the man who conducts the audience on their journey to a dream world.

And how does he do this? First, he must convince himself; he must play the role of the Chairman as an actor convinces himself of the reality of Hamlet's existence. But then, you may argue, Hamlet can be played in so many different ways. Agreed—but so can the Chairman: the trick is to find the manner of performance which will suit your personality. And having said that, I've really said it all, for I don't presume to teach anyone how to acquire personality—the quality to inspire affectionate attention. This book will merely provide a basis of technique, i.e. what to say and when to say it—but *how* to say it is for you to decide.

The only way to become a Chairman is to do it, so I will stop generalizing and get down to cases.

**Costume**

The Chairman should dress as gorgeously as imagination and finances will allow: tails, of course, with black boots, a rose in the buttonhole, a scarlet waistcoat with watch-chain, and white gloves with one or two large sparkling dress-rings over them. He can part his hair in the middle and grow sideboards, but he shouldn't wear a monocle unless he can really handle one, nor should he wear a large moustache unless it really suits him—and if it falls off that precious web of conceit he has been labouring so hard to weave will have been destroyed.

For his entrance, to make it as impressive as possible, he can wear a top hat, cloak and silk scarf, and flourish a cane. If these props are needed by someone else later in the programme, he can put down his cigar and nonchalantly hurl them into the wings before starting his opening patter with a bang of his gavel.

**Opening Patter**

This falls into six sections:
1. He welcomes the audience
2. He tells the audience what they are going to see
3. He introduces himself
4. He introduces the band and/or pianist
5. He takes the audience through the first chorus song
6. He introduces the first item in the programme proper

**The Gavel**

This is his badge of office and should be used to mark the interval, the start of the programme proper after each interval, and, of course, the entrance of each artiste or start of each act. It can also be used to quell any disturbances in the auditorium—or even to bring an artiste to heel, should occasion demand (see page 122).

**The Chairman's Table**

This should be placed opposite the piano, to provide a framework, or if the piano is in the centre, the opposite side to that mainly used by the artistes to make their entrances. If the artistes are using both sides indiscriminately, he should be opposite the stage-manager, in order to be able to signal lighting-changes or to give whatever cues may be necessary—and to signal for assistance in emergencies.

The table should be covered with a scarlet cloth, and have on it the Chairman's notes, a candle in a candlestick, the gavel, cigars, matches (in a silver holder if possible) and an ashtray. If the Chairman prefers to smoke a pipe—he should not smoke cigarettes—it should be a churchwarden or large calabash, and not a short modern briar. Finally, he should have his tankard, ready charged with water or orange squash—not alcohol, since with any luck the patrons will keep him well supplied with beer (see page 120).

By his table will be a large comfortable chair, with cushions to match the tablecloth.

## Patter

I shall not expatiate at length on patter at this point, as the rest of this book is given up to the subject, with suggestions and caveats at the start of each chapter. I have constantly repeated throughout the danger of doing too much patter, since nothing is more wearisome that a Chairman who insists on performing a full sequence of gags between each and every act. Apart from anything else, this habit drags the show out interminably besides lessening the impact of the comics in the programme proper. I once put in a Chairman to deputize for myself for two performances; he put thirty minutes on the show, which did not delight the cast or the management since by the time the final curtain came down the bars were shut.

Should the Chairman do a solo spot? I don't think so. He is on stage for the entire performance, after all, and the audience sees and hears quite enough of him as it is. Nor should he tell jokes as such—leave that to the comics. All the patter in Part II consists of introductions and one-line cracks—there are no funny stories. Remember that whereas a good Chairman can retrieve a bad bill, a bad Chairman can ruin an excellent bill, for if an act is bad it will soon be over, but if the Chairman is under par the audience is stuck with him for the whole evening.

I would advise the neophyte Chairman to write out all his patter in full and learn it like a playscript. He will then be "firm" on his lines, and will be able to depart from them to deal with any heckling or untoward occurrence without being thrown, and to continue smoothly and fluently.

The patter will be well-rounded and convoluted, but not too elaborately so, or else again tedium will set in. For non-comedy items a perfectly straightforward introduction is all that is required; similarly at the completion of an act it is not necessary *always* to try for a laugh. An introduction which is opposed to the style of the act following can sometimes be effective, e.g. for "*I'm Shy Mary Ellen, I'm Shy*" (Francis, Day and Hunter), the Chairman can say, ". . . that prodigal powerhouse of personality and passion, Mr. Joe—Soap!" But as I mention later on, don't overdo the alliteration: there are other ways of being amusing.

Ideally the patter before and after an act should reflect the content of the song, the story of philosophy to be expounded—in short it should generally reflect the act itself. For introductions the gavel should be pounded on to the table or block between the artiste's Christian name and the surname; if the artiste is well known he can be mentioned early in the introduction so that subsequent remarks will be the more appreciated, and his name will again be used to bring him on.

On announcing the interval, the Chairman should bang his gavel and blow out his candle, which will be relit after the interval by the musical director, or by a pretty girl or comic stage-hand. Let the hot air rising from the candle remind the Chairman not to waffle. Keep the patter short and to the point, and when in doubt say nothing at all. If you have to fill in for a difficult scene or costume change, use one of the suggestions under the heading *Fillers*. Usually only a couple of minutes are needed, and these will almost invariably be sufficient. If a longer fill is needed, what about greeting your Birthday or Anniversary celebrants?

Raffles and announcements of birthdays, engagements, wedding anniversaries, etc., can be a frightful bore to the Chairman but are all part of the Music Hall idiom and must not be evaded. A word of welcome to any parties in the audience is a positive gain for the Chairman, since it puts them on his side right from the start. All these aspects of Chairmanship are dealt with the chapters headed "Introductions for Shows" and "Miscellaneous".

Finally, in his opening remarks, the Chairman should never inform the audience that he is "taking them back to those grand spacious days of yesteryear. . . ." They should be there already, and it is his job to see that they stay there.

# INTRODUCTIONS FOR SHOWS

The Chairman should be preceded by the pianist, who lights the candles on the Chairman's table and upon the piano and then commences the overture. Half-way through the final chorus of the overture, the house lights lower and the Chairman appears in the auditorium, dressed in full and magnificent evening dress, complete with white gloves, cloak, silk scarf, topper and cane— and cigar. He processes majestically through the audience, followed by the spotlight, greeting them to left and to right. He mounts to his table, throws his cane into the wings, which is followed by his cloak and topper, picks up his gavel and brings it down with a crash on the final chord of the overture.

## 1 The Opening

My lords, ladies and gentlemen—Good evening! (wait for response) Come along, now, you can and you will do better. My lords, ladies and gentlemen—GOOD EVENING! (wait for response) And welcome to this Cavern of Conviviality, this Emporium of Entertainment, in which the management proudly presents at *enorm* ... (stop and look surprised, then say "Oh, you've seen the show before ...?)

... a conglomerate yet cohesive concretion of consummate competence and considerable craft, carefully contrived to captivate the connoisseur (If you are getting a good reaction, interrupt yourself by saying "I've learnt this so I'm going to say it!"), and to confound the ... er ... to confound the—castigator! .... And that was better out than in!

... a superior and sparkling series of salubrious scenas (pronounced "Shay-ners") and scintillating solos, subtly sequestered into a superlative and stylish symposium

... a decorous yet diverting diffusion of delights, deftly designed to desport the discriminating dilettante and to dumbfound the ... er ... to dumbfound the—detractor!

... an adulatory and absorbing amalgam of accomplished artistes, advantageously arrayed to assay the very acme of admirable

## Your Distinguished Chairman

... er ... admirable—aspirations ... you didn't understand a word I was saying, did you ...? You can tell we're in the Provinces, Maestro ...

... a veritable mammoth production, and anyone who's ever tried to produce a mammoth will know how very difficult that can be

... an enthralling and entrancing embroglio of entertainments egregiously and effectively executed the which to edify and enchant

... a predominance of prestigious performers presenting the prerequisite portion of panache

... a glittering array of divers talents culled from the four corners of the Victoria Embankment (or local)

The artistes appearing tonight have been culled from as far afield as Battersea and Gospel Oak (or local), the securing of whose services has incurred the management in *minimal* expense—anyone out of work at this time of year must be cheap ...

Yes, we have divers surprises and innovations which I know will appeal especially to such an attractive and intelligent audience ...

Prepare for songs and dances of a select and refined variety; for mirth and merriment galore; and prepare in our dramatic interlude to be harrowed to the marrow ... how long is it since you were last harrowed, madam, eh? ... Last Tuesday? Some people have all the luck ...

A small but distinguished audience. ... I see some old familiar faces and some strange faces ... yes, some of them are very strange indeed

I'd like first of all to welcome all our regular patrons—and I trust we are all regular ... are we all regular? Are we all regular? (wait for response) Anyone who isn't see me afterwards and bring your own spoon ...

We ask you to wallow in our customary maudlin nostalgia, as we bring you the songs you love to sing and the jokes you love to hear

I'd like to start by making a little appeal to you all—a little appeal—oh, she's getting her purse out! No, not that kind of an appeal, madam—this is an appeal to laugh as much as you can at the jokes—just to let us know you're still there—you feel such a fool if nobody bothers. So I want to see rows of gleaming teeth ... come on, show us your teeth ... show

us your teeth—no, show 'em, madam, don't hand 'em round!
(No, don't laugh—she's walked here all the way from Barking... must be up the creek!)
I'm delighted to see such a select and fashionable audience here tonight. I understand some of you even come from (local rough district) How nice to see my kind of people here... skint...
May I say how delighted I am to be appearing here in (say wrong town) once again... No? Where? (wait for response, then look at shirt cuff) Sorry, I've got the wrong shirt on
It's so nice to be here in (state town) I like (town) as a whole (hole)
...
I'd like to bid an especially warm welcome to the large party from (local)... she's sitting over there by the bar...
And a warm welcome to the gentleman from Epsom—he's sitting over there drinking his salts... keep the gangway clear over there, won't you?
And to the party of vegetarians from (local), may I just say—moo! (To party) You are from (local)? I have relations there ... I won't say who with...
Ah well, summer draws on...
Here it is, May (or whatever month it happens to be)... time to wash the glasses again...
(For full house) Good to see such a dense crowd here tonight...
(For poor house) A small but alert, intelligent and fashionable audience in tonight... mind you, we have had smaller houses. Oh yes—last week the audience was so small we all got a cab and went to see a show... It was like Aberdeen on a flag day!
Nice to see so many ladies in the house. I always say that an audience without ladies... is like a garden without flowers... (wait for 'Aaah!')... what a creep!
Welcome to the second best way of spending an evening—and if you have to ask what is the best, it's too late.
Good to be here in (*local*)—I've just come back from doing missionary work in (*local rival town*). What a boring place that is! Two bus stops and a cemetery...
(In a large hall) What a big place this is! They don't have a manager—every two years they elect a Mayor.
Good evening, ladies and gentlemen—have I missed anyone out?
Good evening, ladies and gentlemen—that's the rehearsed bit... from now on it's all nerve.
Do your best to laugh at the jokes. If you can't laugh try and force

a little titter ... a little titter here, a little titter there—it all adds up to a big titter. Besides, it lets us know you're still there otherwise we can all go home.

We have a mixed bag for you this evening—she should be here about nine o'clock ...

You've paid your money you might as well enjoy yourselves.

I'm your Chairman for the evening. That's a kind of MC—master of cemeteries.

In this year of grace income tax is threepence in the pound ... you can get drunk for a penny ... dead-drunk for tuppence ... and for a hapenny you can get enough bile beans to keep you on the move for a month OR and knicker elastic is a farthing a leg.

Of course, I've been to (*local*) once before but it was shut.

I've got digs in (*local posh area*) ... Oh, yes, I like to stay where the big knobs hang out. I said to my landlady "It's very nice round here but you must have trouble with the rates." She said "Oh, we don't have rates—only maice ..."

Good ladies, evening and gentlemen—I knew I should have rehearsed that ...

Good evening, opponents ...

Any parties in tonight? Oh—are you having your annual do?

(To party of ladies) Hello, girls, enjoying yourselves? Why, what are you doing ...? So you're all in the club, are you ...?

Here we are, all ready to enjoy an evening of fun and frivolity without a trace of vulgarity ... that's ruined the evening before we've started ...

(After concerted opening item) Well, that's our company—did you like the look of them ...? That's all you're going to get so you might as well make the best of it ... damn cheek ...

## 2 Introduction of Chairman by Himself

My name is ——, don't bother to stand, just nod, and I have the pleasure to be your Chairman for the evening. I come from a very aristocratic family as you can probably tell. My grandfather was a peer ... and grandmother had kidney trouble as well ...

I've recently been appearing in the Mecca of the Music Hall: the Hippodrome, High Street, Mecca ... no, seriously, *this* theatre is known as the Mecca of the Music Halls throughout the profession—on pay day we face east. Pay day! That's a laugh—if this was China, I'd be picketed by coolies. Still, you get a nice tan from the lights . . .

I am (give height); I weigh (give weight) . . . for any further queries, ladies, send a stamped addressed envelope to the stage door, (local) Theatre . . .

What a lovely theatre this is . . . it'll be nice when it's finished . . . there's one thing about working at the (local) Theatre—from here you can only go up . . .

(If you fluff) I'm breaking these teeth in for the dog. OR That's the last time I get my teeth by mail order.

I'm working under a grave disadvantage tonight—I'm sober.

I got out of a sick bed to be here tonight—my girl-friend's got flu.

My name is ――― . . . thank you for that burst of indifference.

Hands up all those who've never seen me before . . . hands up all those who don't care if they never see me again . . .! (A forest of hands always goes up) . . . oh, I can see we're going to be friends . . .

Years ago I used to have a lady friend here. A gorgeous little thing she was—I was wild about here! I adored her to distraction! I'd have followed her to the ends of the earth . . . well, I would have done but she moved to (*rival town or notoriously dreary local area*).

This is a return engagement for me—I was here yesterday.

(If playing a return date after many years) It's eight years since I was last here, so this is in the nature of a return engagement . . .

Nice to be here. I used to have relations in (*local*). I won't say who with but it was a wonderful summer.

I once spent six months here finishing a book. I'm a very slow reader.

I like (*local*). I like the way it's laid out . . . I don't know when it died but I like the way it's laid out . . .

Welcome to (*local*)—City of Sin, Scandal and High-Living . . .

Ensure that local dignitaries, with their correct titles, are mentioned in the opening patter. For a one-night stand always ask the organisers of the evening whether anyone in particular should be mentioned—the association's chairman, the firm's managing director, the club's sports champion, etc., etc., etc. A little homework in this respect pays dividends as it shows the audience that the Chairman both knows and cares about them. Be very careful with jokes to specialised audiences, i.e. golfing jokes at a golf club—they will almost certainly have heard them before.

**3 Introduce Band and/or Pianist** (see page 56)

**4 Announce First Song-sheet Chorus** (see page 62)

After first chorus song by the Chairman, he bangs his gavel, the house lights lower again, and he says, "Which brings us—and not before time—to the programme proper . . . the programme improper will be given in the church hall on Sunday morning . . . I have to laugh myself and I'm in it! . . . After banging gavel sharply and wincing, look at it and say "Look at that—I'm ruining my knocker! It is a shame . . ."

During this opening patter, the Chairman should also be on the *qui vive* for Latecomers (see page 60) and, of course, Heckling (see page 101).

# AUDIENCE PARTICIPATION

These routines can be used as part of the Chairman's introduction, with the exception of the first, which is better left till later in the evening—possibly directly after an interval or as a filler. (See p. 114)

You will be fascinated to learn, I know, that there is to be built in the High Street (or local) a new *public house*! . . . (if response is poor, the Chairman can say, "What? Are we all teetotal?" And then repeat from the start. This should produce the required cheers) Unfortunately, I am sorry to tell you that in this public house there will only be *one bar* . . .   (groans)
   —a mile long!   (cheers)
   —But there will only be one barmaid . . .   (groans)
   —For each customer!   (cheers)
   —There will be no pint pots . . .   (groans)
   —Only quarts!   (cheers)
   —And the beer will be diluted . . .   (groans)
   —With whisky!   (cheers)
   —But the bar will close at ten o'clock . . .   (groans)
   —In the morning!   (cheers)

Thank you very much indeed—well done!

Hands up all those who've never been to a Music Hall before? . . . Isn't it hell?

To those of you who may never have visted a Music Hall before, perhaps I should explain that it is customary to demonstrate your approval of the artistes' efforts not only by applauding and shouting, but also by stamping your feet . . . shall we have a short rehearsal? Very well, after three—three! (demonstrate stamping) Mind the lady's corns, sir . . . once again, now . . . (stamp again) . . . thank you so much—we're having a lot of trouble with cockroaches this summer/at present . . .

In order to engender the atmosphere of *esprit de corps* so essential to the success of a Music Hall evening, may I ask you, upon a count of three and not before, to turn to your neighbour on your right, then to your neighbour on your left, and say "Hello!" or "How are you?" or "Ugh!", whichever you may deem to be apt . . . after three—three! (conduct the audience) Hello . . . ! How are you . . . ? What, no ugh? (pull "bad smell" face) . . . all very friendly this evening. Well, now, having thoroughly embarrassed the entire audience, may I continue with . . .

In this year of Grace we can hear the gaslights *hissing* . . . (put hand to ear to encourage audience to hiss) . . . yes, that's a sound I've heard a few times . . . we can hear all the hansom-cabs *clip-clopping* up and down the streets . . . (wait for clip-clopping) . . . and we can see and hear all the people *scurrying* to the Music Hall! . . . (wait for whatever noise audience makes) . . . yes, that's a difficult one . . .

If the chairman's opening chorus is *"Daisy Belle"* or a similar gentle waltz encourage the audience to sway from side to side. Perhaps a 'Sway Leader' in the front can be appointed: if there is a centre aisle two leaders can be appointed and each side sway in different directions. Capital can be made out of a leader if she is a pretty girl or if he is a well-known local personality or eccentrically dressed.

Hands up all those gentlemen sitting with their wives . . . hands up all those gentlemen sitting with someone *else's* wife . . . hands up all those gentlemen who'd *like* to be sitting with someone else's wife . . . yes, always the most hands go up on that . . .

Music Hall started in London, of course, so let's all pretend to be Cockneys. Gentlemen, I'd like you to turn to the lady next to you and say, "Wotcher, ducks! 'Ow are yer?" Shall we try that? . . . Splendid! Now, ladies, wasn't that nice? And I'd like you to respond in your most charming manner, "Mind your own bleedin' business" . . . oh, very Roedean . . .

Anyone from (*local*)? Your coach has broken down OR isn't coming back.

To girl: think of a number between one and six . . . five? Sorry, you're wrong. Take your clothes off.

Can you hear me at the back? (*Yes*!) That's funny—most people's ears are at the side . . .

Can you hear me at the back? (*No*!) I'm not surprised at one and ninepence . . . never mind, comrades, come the revolution you'll all be at the front . . . (to front) I don't know what you're laughing at—you'll all be at the back!

# INTRODUCTIONS FOR BAND AND PIANIST

Musicians are always extremely popular with audiences, and virtually anything the Chairman says about them is sure to be well received. If there are just two or three in the band each name can be announced, leaving the leader until last. Don't overdo the patter at this point: the opening remarks plus the Chairman's first chorus should not total more than six minutes. Always address the leader/accompanist as "Maestro" or "Madame" if a lady. See my *Musical Joke Book* (Fentone).

## 1 Band

Here they are—Manuel and his Music of the Middens
None of 'em could pass a dope test
 ... and to accompany the entire performance we are honoured to have in the pit—and that's where they belong—the Stockwell (*or local*) Stompers ... each and every one of them is a soloist in his own right—as you could probably tell from the overture
 ... and to accompany the entire performance in the gutter—they're used to it—we have Maestro—and his Tepid Two ...
We should have had a quintet but the other two were refused bail
Our ensemble comes to us direct from a Promenade Concert at the Royal Albert—Memorial
This is the only band where the melody is carried by the drummer
 ... here we have the grand augmented (*local*) chamber ensemble
 ... we're all potty here, you know
 ... hello, the band's laughing—that's a bad sign ... if you want to laugh buy a ticket like everyone else ... mind you, it's only fair if they laugh at my jokes. I laugh at their playing ...
(Again if band laughs) Hello, I'm making the staff laugh
Tonight they'll be playing as never before ... in tune
You may have seen them before—by the War Memorial on Saturday afternoons (*or local*)
They also play for Irish dances under the name of Knuckles O'Reilly and his Ditch Diggers
At one performance the Maestro fell off his rostrum—he went brass over oboe.

# Your Distinguished Chairman

Wonderful news! Our trumpeter's wife has just given birth to a bouncing baby boy! So will the proud father please rise? (All the band stand)

We should have had a four-piece band but they only knew three pieces

The Maestro is responsible for the orchestral arrangements for this performance. Yes, he has personally seen to all his band's parts.

## 2 Instrumentalists

He used to play the bass tuba but he wore out his pucker

On the bull fiddle we have Mr – – –. He used to play one fifteen feet tall and that's a lot of bull

Then we have Mr – – – playing his hot trumpet. He only stole it this afternoon ...

On the clarinet we have Mr – – –, LRAM and bar

Mr – – – is on the slide-trombone and DDT spray

On the fiddle we have Mr – – – who spent three years in Paris under Madame Fifi Le Bonbon, which accounts for his tendency to play flat

He plays a wonderful instrument. Four more payments and it's his

Here we have the Van Gogh of the saxophone **(or other instrument)** ... he hasn't got much of an ear

**(For drummer)** Here we have the Tetrazzini of the triangle ... What a drummer! He's got the biggest bongoes in the business. He beats as he sweeps as he plays **(can also be used for pianist)**

He used to play the cello but the spike kept making a hole in his jacket

He used to play the fiddle but his beer kept sliding off

He used to play the organ but someone shot his monkey

What a guitarist! Known to his peers as Orpheus in the Underpants.

**(For lady musician)** Wonderful musician, that lady. She's been under some of the finest conductors in Europe

She tells me she has often played at the Prom Concerts. "Oh?" I said, "Sir Henry Wood?" She said, "All the time if I'd let him ..."

**(For lady brass player)** Here we have on the trumpet our lady brass, if you'll pardon the expression

## 3 Pianist

**(After florid piece of playing)** This is a fine time to practise!

Here he is, on the piano and on the wagon

Here he is on a surety of five pounds and with his horse securely chained to the railings outside ... you will take your gloves off tonight, won't you?

He's just had his instrument tuned so he's feeling rather highly strung. Never mind, Maestro, we're all on your side ... so far.

Here is our Madame Maestro—I don't like to call her Maestress, somehow

Give us a quick archipelago, Maestro ... (wait for long arpeggio up the keyboard) ... beautiful! But does he go down ... ?

**(After announcing pianist)** The Maestro won't stand up–he's pawned his trousers OR he's got his feet in a mustard bath—well, it has been a bit nippy lately

He not only plays the pianoforte but also the harmonium, the euphonium, the pandemonium and the B flat hoover

At a very early age he was known to play on the linoleum

The Maestro is no mean musician—buy him a drink and he's anybody's—he's played under Toscanini. Used to give him piggyback rides

Here on our grand Italian grand pianoforte—the strings are made of spaghetti—is Maestro --- who was as I expect you remember the 1896 Olympic Gold Medallist in the keyboard sprint

The Maestro is also a composer. He's just completed his latest work: a concerto for hoover and wet flannel

Here is that celebrated refugee from Wurlitzer's ... known to his friends in the musical trade as Sledgehammer Sid OR Piledriver Pete ... late of the Mount Zion Jug-Blowing Rascals

During this opening chorus we shall be accompanied by the *entire* maestro

As always he'll be playing with feeling—feeling for the right notes

I won't say he's thick but he thinks a semi-breve is a cold in the head

Loves classical music, does our Maestro. Last night I said to him, "What do you think of Handel's Largo?" He said, "I never drink anything else."

And last night he did a classical piece in A flat

Here we have our customary nine-piece orchestra, consisting of eight absentees and a pianist

The Maestro used to play in a sextet. The other five were all girls and you can't get a sexier tet than that

The Maestro appears tonight by courtesy of money

Now I must introduce the man who will be spending the entire performance earnestly bent over his upright OR his magnificent instrument

Here is the man who will be accompanying, and from time to time overtaking, the entire company

And now I have the honour to introduce our *orchestra* ... last week he was playing the Palladium but tonight he's playing the piano

A versatile man, our Maestro—he's also a qualified plumber, you know. Nothing he doesn't know about wiping a joint

He went to the Royal Academy of Music ... pity they were shut

Here now, tickling the ivories with gay abandon and anything else within reach ...

The Maestro is a very distinguished musician. He's a veritable virtuoso on the virginals—and he's prepared to prove it

Here's a man who lives music, eats music and sleeps music. If only he could *play* music!

The Maestro will play not only the black notes but also the white notes, and if the performance is anything like last night he will also be playing the cracks in between

The Maestro will not only play with the right hand but also with the left hand, and even, should occasion arise, with both hands at one and the same time! Well done, sir.

To accompany the performance we have the (*local*) Light Orchestra which plays as one man—and here is that one man

Here is our own one-man pianist

Here he is, a bachelor of music and father of ten

Are you well, Maestro? (Yes, thank you) Are you sober! (Just about) Well, that makes a change. No, the Maestro recently had a nasty accident—he caught his crochet on a stave.

# LATECOMERS

Most latecomers of course arrive during the Chairman's opening patter and so the gags in this section will mostly be of use at that time. Again, do not use too many otherwise the joke will get tedious. Other latecomers can perhaps be caught during the Chairman's introductions of acts in the programme proper, or after the intervals. It is nice if the follow-spot can pick up the people the Chairman is addressing.

Good evening, how nice of you to come. We did wait for you, but we thought we'd have the show first and eat afterwards . . .

Good evening, so *there* you are! Would you like us to start again? (if "Yes!" is shouted back) Very well, that'll be an extra £5 3s 6d . . . OR repeat everything you've said at breakneck speed

Are you sure you've come to the right meeting? . . . You *have* come to be saved?

**(to woman in fur coat)** I like the coat . . . when do you feed it?

Do you have a note? . . . A fiver will do . . .

Do you have a seat? . . . Good . . . and somewhere to put it?

**(to people standing)** Don't you have a seat? Well, keep your coat buttoned up and no-one will notice . . .

**(to girl with man)** Is that your hubby or your hobby?

Don't be embarrassed—everyone's looking at you. (If this is to a single woman and she says, "I'm not embarrassed," the Chairman can say) Ooh, the brazen hussy! (If a man gives the same reply, say) *I* would be in that suit . . .

**(to person struggling along row)** Keep going—you're on the last lap

**(two women)** Evening, ladies . . . trade bad?

**(two men)** Good evening . . . you two gentlemen together? . . . I see . . .

**or** Good evening, gentlemen . . . no luck in (local red light district)?

**(to late party)** Ah, I see Sir Thomas Lipton's Tea Party has just arrived

**or** Ah, here's the party from (local lunatic asylum or primary school)

## Your Distinguished Chairman

**(late couple)** Why are you two late? What have you been up to? Couldn't wait, eh? Like animals, some people.
**(late couple)** Good evening, sir—is this a pleasure trip or is that your wife?
or Is that the wife with you, sir? ... Novelty night ...
**(to man with two women)** Good evening, sir ... you're doing well ... what have you got that I haven't got?
**(to woman with two men)** Good evening, madame ... having a private party after the show?
**(when latecomers arrive just before the interval, the Chairman should make a great fuss of them)** Did your tandem have a puncture? ... I know how it is ... all settled now ... that's it, take your coat off, dear ... got your song-sheets? ... all right ... Ladies and Gentlemen—the INTERVAL!
Did your horse throw a shoe? What a shame ...
You must get yourself mechanized ...
It's beauty and the beast.
**(to audience when party of latecomers enters obtrusively)** Take no notice—just pretend you're enjoying yourselves.
**(to bald man)** Would you mind moving back, sir? The light from your head is shining right in my eyes.
**(to bearded man)** I like the beard. Haven't I seen your face on a packet of Players? Or a packet of something?
**(to late party)** Tillings are so unreliable these days ...
—And about time!
You didn't mind us starting without you?
Is that the wife? Oh no, she's got a box of chocolates.
We nearly marked you absent
A bit early for tomorrow night's show, aren't you?
**(to girl in revealing dress)** Don't get hiccups, will you? We'll have a whip-round to get the rest of the dress.
**(when people stand up to let latecomer pass)** Don't stand up—make him jump ... Never mind, you're on the last lap.
Don't be embarrassed—everyone's looking at you.
What a lot of latecomers this evening! More late entries than an Irish orchestra.
A pity you couldn't manage a clean shirt for the occasion.
I hate that tie.
Nice to know tailors still have a sense of humour.
Are you alone or is there anyone else in that suit?

# SONG-SHEETS

Song-sheets should be provided if at all possible—and it follows that there must be enough light to read them by. Therefore the house lights should be brought up to one-third or one-half whenever the Chairman announces the song-sheet number. Always mention the number at the beginning of an announcement or the artiste's entrance will be ruined by a rustling of song-sheets. To shouts of "We can't see!" you reply "Our estimable stage-manager will be bringing the house-lights up at the appropriate moment—never fear!"

It is perhaps best to allow the soloist to perform the first chorus on his or her own; the house-lights can come up and the Chairman start singing lustily himself for the second and subsequent choruses; the lights to go out for the verses, unless the verses are very short.

The first song-sheet chorus should be conducted by the Chairman alone; sometimes the Chairman does several songs at the introduction of the show, but this makes the opening too drawn-out. One chorus, perhaps sung twice, is sufficient.

### 1 For the Chairman's Opening Spot

Now I will ask you to take up your song-sheets, provided free gratis and for nothing by a beneficent and benevolent management at *enormous* expense.

Now I will ask you to take up your hymn-sheets . . . do you all have your hymn-sheets? . . . (wait for response) . . . and can you all read? . . . (wait for response which is usually "No!") . . . I should never have left Woolworth's (or local store) . . . and I will ask you to turn your collective attention to number N inscribed thereon, a little number I wrote myself under the name of Stephen Foster, and entitled (give song title) . . . perhaps we should have a little tune-up first—can we have a suitable tune-up note, Maestro? An "A" perhaps? (note from piano) Hasn't he got a lovely touch? You want to watch your wallets down there, I can tell you . . . (sings note) La, la, la . . . may I hear you

## Your Distinguished Chairman

all?... La, laaaa... (hold long note and encourage audience to do the same)... from here it looks like a dentist's nightmare
**or** Is there a vet in the house? Very well, a quick archipelago then, Maestro, and away we go

**(after chorus has been sung once)** I think we need perhaps to clear our throats... (cough and encourage audience to do the same. This is usually done very enthusiastically)... with as much delicacy as we can muster... right, once again and this time sing with lust and fervour—or either, depending on your state of health...

**(after second time)** Very good indeed, and may I ask you when we come to subsequent choruses to sing with gusto—evening, Gus, there he is in the front row

May I also ask you to oblige with the refrain from spitting...

I now ask you to turn to number N, hymns ancient and decrepit...

I sincerely hope that subsequent choruses will bring an improvement in volume and in quality—you're not in a place of entertainment now, you know...

I see we have here a choir representing most of London's postal districts

I understand we have in tonight a party of midwives... they can always be relied upon for a fine delivery...

Come along now, let's raise the roof—it doesn't belong to us...

**(When audience is eating)** Now, I want you all to stop masticating...

I want you all to open your vowels... and catch me on the upthrust

Can you all read? (No!) Can you all count? (No!) So much for compulsory education... we start with number one on your race-cards—song-sheets—a song I wrote myself while waiting for a laugh last Wednesday afternoon...

Thank you, Maestro—we shan't need a key, we'll let ourselves in

I want you to sing up or I'll be coming round with a big whip... you'd enjoy that wouldn't you? Funny people in (local)

This tune may be unfamiliar but you'll soon pick it up. I understand you're experienced at picking up hereabouts

I want each and every one of you to open your mouth and really throw yourself into it

Come on, now, I want big breaths

Please do not refrain from the refrain

**(After tune-up)** I've just seen more bridgework than Brunel

Did you ever wish you'd never started something?
Sometimes I think Beethoven was lucky being deaf
I couldn't hear a thing. You'll have to sing up—I'm a little deaf. It's all that applause, you know
The lady who sings the best will have the privilege of escorting me home after the performance ... I'm staying in (local black spot)—it's a lovely place at this time of year
The gentleman who sings the best will receive a wonderful prize—a camping holiday for two on a traffic island in the Great West Road (*or local black spot*).
The prize for the best singer in the audience is a wonderful—(look at notes)—diving suit ... (look again) divan suite ...
The first prize is a ten pound tin of rat poison and a year's supply of rats OR a season ticket to (local) crematorium OR a week's holiday in (local black spot). The second prize is *two* weeks' holiday in (same local black spot)
We have wonderful prizes to encourage you to sing. The first prize is a teapot, the second prize is a coffee-pot and the third prize a pistol. OR The first prize is a parasol, the second prize a camisole and the third prize an Arsenal season ticket
I want you to sing or just take off your shoes and hum
(**To woman taking coat off**) That's right, dear, spread a little happiness ... have a night out
(**To man who sings loud high note during 'tune-up'** I'm glad I don't have to do your laundry
Thank you, Maestro. Give us a local A ... now, start pedalling, vicar, and away we go
Do you have your song sheets? Would you care to wave your white forms at me? ... thank you, it does get a little stuffy in here. We did have air-conditioning but the bat died.


## 2 For Later in the Programme

This is a somewhat raucous number, so may I advise you to loose what needs to be loosed, and adjust what needs to be adjusted ...
The gentleman who sings this chorus the best will be presented with a vintage bottle of Hong Kong sherry, and the lady who sings the best will get a kiss from him on the piano ... we take the candle off first so you'll be all right ...
This particular chorus is not on your song-sheets, since we felt it

would be an impertinence for such an audience of Music Hall aficionados...

**(when the Chairman announces a number which is not on the song-sheet, and the audience can be seen looking for it)** Your assistance is not required for this number... (if said with charm this always gets a laugh) . . . but we shall be calling upon your services again later on, never fear . . .

**(when chorus is just a repeat of the title, as with** "*Ta Ra Ra Boom De Ay*") This chorus is not on your song-sheets as it is merely a titular refrain . . . and what, you are asking yourselves, is a titular refrain? . . . in a titular refrain, you just have to keep abreast of the artiste . . .

# INTRODUCTIONS FOR GENTLEMEN

As with the introductions for ladies, the Chairman should not be too verbose. The introduction should reflect the manner and matter of the performance to follow; with straight ballads just an announcement of the lyricist and composer, followed by the title —and of course the singer—is sufficient. Be careful with comic introductions that the wrong impression is not given, i.e. a gentle humorous number should not be given an introduction which suggests a knock-down, drag-out slapstick act. Always use the prefix "Mister".

Here he is:
that well-known bon viveur and specialist in stage-waits . . .
    your friend and his . . .
the man who put the Strange into Strangeways . . .
the last of the big-time losers . . .
that elegant if egregious entertainer . . .
that celebrated buffo-vocalist . . .
that dishevelled, despicable and dissolute desperado . . .
the man with the winning smile and the losing face . . .
that *sans pareil* of sartorial splendour . . .
that prodigal power-house of personality and passion . . .
that distinguished man about town, notary public and shoes repaired while you wait . . .
that well-known deb's delight and commode renovator . . .
that well-known socialite and midden cleaner . . .
that stark, staring, stagnant, stage-door Johnny . . .
**(for Scottish number)** that eminent haggis renovator and bag-pipe trapper . . .
that celebrated commodi—comedian . . .
that paragon of perfect poise and panache . . .
**(for pirate number)** a man steeped in thuggery, skulduggery and bu-cancering . . .
the man of whom it was once said
the man who has been described as one of the country's rising

young stars; and here is the man who said it . . .
your own, and you can keep him . . .
the man who recently caused a sensation at the Electric Theatre, Barrow-in-Furness (or local)—he spilt his beer over the manager's dicky
the man whose rendering of this number makes Harry Champion (or whoever) look even better . . .
**(for song and dance)** the man who put the terps into terpsichore . . .
the man whose performance of this song has been compared to Caruso's (or whoever) but not very favourably/often . . .
all the way from his yacht on the Hackney Marshes (or local) . . .
You've heard of Whistler's mother. Here's Frankenstein's father...
Here's a man who really wants to make it big . . . so let's give him a helping hand up . . .
Mr N has recently appeared in East India . . . Dock Road . . .
Mr N has appeared before all the crowned heads of Europe, and also before the President of the United—Dairies.
Now we present a man:
who is a walking advertisement to the efficacy of Bob Martin's . . .
of singular accomplishments and attainments—mostly of a dubious nature
**(for Magic Act)** who will astonish and amaze us with his feats of legerdemain, wizardry and presdigitation—which is almost as hard to say as to do. Ladies and gentlemen, that mage of mystery, that master of magic, that Maestro of mumchance, Professor N! OR So here now giving us all the mystery of the Orient—not to mention Tottenham Hotspur and the Arsenal—is . . .
for a full list of whose vices we have neither the time nor the stomach. Suffice it to say that he both smokes! and—(looks both ways) drinks! . . . Here, then, soiling the boards of the (local) Theatre, is . . .
who has just completed a record-breaking run at the White City stadium—the cinders were still hot
who comes to us straight from a season in the Great Hall of the Eddystone lighthouse OR Royal Opera House, Sark.
who has just completed a sensationally successful season at Burridges Cocoa Rooms, Balls Pond Road . . . (or local)
who comes to us direct from a whirlwind tour of the Rotherhithe Tunnel . . . (or local)
who comes to us direct from the darkest stews of Neasden (or

local) where the revelry, not to say deviltry, has been known to continue until nine *p.m.*!

who has just completed a season at Billingsgate Fish Market . . . always a strong act . . .

whose dark sideburns have tickled the ladies' fancies in three continents to my certain knowledge . . .

**(for comedy military number)** Mr N is an ex-officer who served with conspicuous lack of gallantry in the Post Office Hussars, before he was cashiered for some unfortunate dealings with the mails . . . (males) . . . However, here he is now with (song title) in which he will delineate some of the highlights, or should I say lowlights, of an exceptionally murky career . . .

Here, with all the febrile and feverish ferocity of a forceful and (to front row) am I splashing you? I'm so sorry . . . of a forceful and frantic four-flusher, is . . .

**(straight song)** Once again Mr N will occupy our attentions, this time with the ever-popular ballad (title), so may I ask for the warmest possible welcome, if you please, for the elegance, grace and manly charm of Mr N!

**(for comic parson act)** I am told that you here (local) are all fervent and enthusiastic church-goers, so I know you will be delighted to learn that we have persuaded the Vicar of St Moribund's OR St Cuthbert's-on-the-Verge to give us an improving address. Ladies and gentlemen, a warm but respectful welcome, if you please, for the Reverend N!

**(for cod recitation)** We are honoured to welcome to the podium tonight the eminent Shakespearean tragedian, Mr N, parts one and two, who has graciously consented to favour us with . . .

or And now, I proudly announce the name which causes hushed whispers and mordant sighs wherever men of sagacity and sensitivity foregather. Mr N!

Having been forcibly ejected from all the flop-houses and Salvation Army hostels in the vicinity, it is with not a little trepidation that I now announce . . .

**(for "*My Old Dutch*")** We are privileged now to witness the fourteenth farewell appearance of that dirty old—grand old man of the Halls, Mr N, who will now oblige with that grand old tear-jerker: "*My Old Dutch*", number—on your song-sheets . . .

**(for autobiographical song)** Mr N will now recall some of the more bizarre episodes of his rather bizarre life under the collective title of "*Bang Went The Chance of a Lifetime*" (or whatever).

## Your Distinguished Chairman

Mr N has led a strange and varied existence, having at various times been bag-maker to Mr Gladstone, greaser-in-chief to the late Captain Webb, and inventor of the gas telephone

**(for number played in naval uniform)** ... in this naughty nautical number, Able Seaman N now brings his able body into view with...

**(for patter act)** Take a firm grip on your beer, your wallet and your wife—in that order—as we are now to be exposed to the bold, brash and brassy—but not I trust bawdy—banter of Mr N!

Mr N is of course a corduroy bass of repute ...

It's been a long time since we had a really good singer/comic on the programme, and our next act is no exception ...

...he of the gimlet eye, the finely chiselled nostrils and the hammer toes ...

... he of the hawk eyes and the crow's feet ...

Mr N was going to sing "*My Love Lies Sleeping*" with a male voice choir, but they missed the bus ...

I'm not sure what he intends to do when he gets here, but I suspect that when he's finished we shall wish he hadn't bothered ...

Here now, flashing his wit for all to behold ...

Mr N is an artiste of the first water—in fact he's a big drip

Mr N of course comes from the select residential neighbourhood of Cockfosters (or local) where all the big knobs hang out ... you thinking of moving, are you, dear?

**(for** "*Turned Up*"—Feldman's) Dickens lovers among us—and who is not?—will remember how Mr Micawber was always waiting for something to turn up. Something *has* turned up for our next artiste ...

We now welcome a man of universal acclaim and Boots' (or local) surgical appliance counter ...

He's been entertaining at Buckingham Palace, I understand—well, he said something about being detained for Her Majesty's Pleasure

And now, it's the lovely—

He'll be favouring us with a touching little song touchingly sung, and if I know Mr—he'll be touching me for a quid after the performance

Here now, from all the well-known Music and Billiard Halls in (local) is ...

He has just finished in Scotland. Boy, is he finished in Scotland ...?

He's always been very sophisticated but he tells me he's been taking the tablets and he's much better now
His act is like the soup du jour—you never know what to expect
Here now, trying to keep his end up
He can always be relied upon to make his mark—I only hope we can wipe it off
Of rising eminence
It's the up and coming
The man with the strapping physique ... unfortunately the strap broke
When they made him they broke the mould, which is why he's known as the mouldiest act in the business
He takes his part well—no-one else would touch it with a bargepole
That dapper and debonair delineator of doleful ditties
He is known to Music Hall aficionados as something of a *cult* ... no, he really is a *brick* ...
After his first number we hoped he'd gone home, but here he is again—this might be a good opportunity to water the horses
Here he is, champing at the bit—I wouldn't mind a bit myself holding his own, if you'll pardon the expression
to tell us a little about himself, and believe me a little goes a very long way
with the courage of his many convictions
with a smile, a song and a-ppliance
In the fine rosy flush of asphyxia
direct from a long engagement and a short marriage
This chap really knows his onions—and his act's a load of tripe, too
I don't want to be rude about his voice, but when he sings deaf people won't even watch his lips moving
He's just come back from Australia—he has to go further and further afield to find work
He's the only comic I know who gets his material from the Dead Sea Scrolls OR The Rosetta Stone
We've seen him many times but he's pleaded for one more chance
We've seen him sing some songs and tell some jokes, so here he is, that half-singer and half-wit
His face may not be familiar but his material certainly is

## Your Distinguished Chairman

Now we come to no less an artiste than Mr --- and believe me, there are few lesser artistes than Mr ---
Here, direct from the Abattoir, Aberystwyth ... he really slayed 'em there
He's just finished a Music Hall in the North of England and now he's come to finish it off down here (adjust to suit)
One of the finest comics in the country. Rotten in the city but great in the country
Here he is, saved in the nick of time from the taxidermist
Now we come to an old drinking song sung by an old drunkard
**(For Scots act)** He's a canny performer—he cannae sing, he cannae dance
**(For speciality act)** Mr --- presents a feat unparalleled since the discovery of chloroform
Here's a man I'm always happy to shake warmly by the throat
His ballad singing is known and feared along the south coast
We've heard a lot about him, so now let's hear his side
Some people sing for money, Mr --- does it for spite
Tonight Mr --- will demonstrate a further facet of his miniscular talent
Let's meet and greet the late and great
**(For The Marrow Song)** He's a keen gardener, so here with green fingers and matching teeth is
Mr --- comes from a long line of bachelors
Mr --- has just returned from a tour of Arabian harems! But his tour was curtailed—they found he wasn't cut out for that class of work
With this act anything can happen but probably won't
Here he is, once seen and never remembered (OR) once seen, soon forgotten
He has a useful singing voice—well, it kept him out of the Army
Now we come to one of the better cheaper acts
He comes to us direct from his usual job as a crossing-sweeper on Horse Guards Parade ... heavy work

See also General Introductions (page 84) and Duet Introductions (page 94)

# EXITS FOR GENTLEMEN

A one-liner is usually sufficient; the suggestions below should not stop the Chairman endeavouring to think up his own—ideally all his remarks should relate to the content and/or style of the performance which has just finished. It is advisable for the Chairman to check his patter with the artistes concerned, to ensure that he says nothing which they might consider objectionable. Experienced Music Hall artistes may have their own suggestions to make, which puts the Chairman on unassailable ground. If something untoward has happened during the act, it is a mistake to mention it during the exit patter—the audience will have forgotten the incident and wonder what the Chairman is talking about. However, if something obviously unintended occurs right at the end of the act, i.e. if an artiste working with a cane drops it as he or she exits, the Chairman can say, "Thank you, Mr N/Miss N ... that'll teach you not to work with a cane until you are able ..."

If, however, something occurs during an act *which the artiste doesn't notice*, and which is distracting the audience, it is advisable for the Chairman to interrupt the act to put a stop to the distraction if he can. I was once taking the chair at the Players' Theatre, Charing Cross, when Miss Sheila Matthews was performing, beautifully as always, her medley of Ada Reeve songs. One of Miss Matthew's hair-pins had come loose and was hanging down to one side of her coiffeur, swinging and glinting in the lights. This distraction was, I could tell, spoiling a very fine act, so at a suitable pause in the music I moved forward and extracted the hair-pin. At the conclusion of the act she came over to me and held out her hand, which I took and kissed. I was then able to make play with the hair-pin, saying, "I shall keep this in my bosom for evermore," and the situation had been retrieved. For the record, Miss Matthews afterwards thanked me and agreed that I had done the right thing.

Mr N appears by kind permission of the:
    Burgomaster of Chigwell Halt (or local)
    **or** Governors of Rowton House
    **or** Governor of Wormwood Scrubs
    **or** Warden of Victoria Embankment
    **or** Head Master of (local lunatic asylum)

## Your Distinguished Chairman

Mr N.is a bachelor of this parish—stud fee 3s 6d

Mr N's talents have been remarked on far and wide . . . some say the farther the better

Mr N was of course the first man ever to go *up* Niagara Falls in a barrel . . .

Mr N really throws himself into a song. Next week he will delight us with *"Old Father Thames"*

Mr N is a man of many parts, some of which:
are no longer manufactured
**or** have never seen the light of day, and frankly we think it's better that way

Thank you, Mr N—a fine artiste and a wonderful person to boot

Thank you, Mr N, we'll let you know

Mr N is very shy and modest—but then he's got a lot to be modest about

Mr N is an artiste of great integrity—in fact I can personally vouch for the sensitivity of his scruples

Mr N is a man whose name is a household word:
if you come from that sort of a household
**or** but it's not a word I care to use in mixed company

Mr N is the man of whom it was once said, "If music be the food of love—pass the bicarb!"

Mr N is the man of whom it has often been said

Mr N has a house full of old masters and not a few mistresses

He's got an eye for the girls . . . that's about all he has got

He may not be funny but he's lovable

Girls go out with him by the dozens—it's safer that way . . .

Mr N is now ready to receive a limited number of pupils for his weight-lifting and physical culture classes

Mr N's make-up was by Plaster of Paris

Mr N is now available for children's parties and masonics

Mr N is available for clinical examination after the performance . . .

**(after black-face number)** Thank you, Mr N, and good luck with the Lifebuoy . . .

**(after tramp number)** Thank you, Mr N who was, you may remember, the Tailor and Cutter's Choice for Man of the Year, 1864

**(after comic parson act)** Of course, I'm a pillar of the church myself. Well, more of a flying buttress really—always on the outside

That was Mr – – – who is, of course, the current glue-sniffing champion of (local)

(After 'corny gag' act) He's always so loyal to his material

Thank you for that conducted tour of the joke museum
There he goes, trying for a comeback yet again
He was educated at Harrow—Pauper's Academy
How's that for a triumph of nerve over talent?
Thank you for that—whatever it was
We're all so pleased for Mr ---. He was telling us just before the show that he has signed a contract for a very prestigious summer season on the Goodwin Sands ... have pompoms can swim *OR* playing twice daily
Last time he told those jokes here we had to get in an exorcist
He has just spent six months at the Savoy Hotel—looking for the gents
He also does bird impressions—he eats worms
He told us he did farmyard impressions, but we decided against that when we found out he didn't do the sounds, he did the smells
(After 'tumult' act) Another subtle and understated performance there from Mr ---
He has a vast and enormous repertoire and having shared a dressing-room with him on occasions I'm in a position to know just how vast and enormous it is
He also does a marvellous stage wait
There he goes, still trying to keep his end up
a walking advertisement for the art of the embalmer
He's always so full of beans—I'm glad I'm not sharing a dressing-room with him
Some performers may be one in a million, but he was won in a raffle
He's a self-made man, which is a good trick if you can do it
He likes to describe himself as a self-made man, thus relieving the Almighty of a grave responsibility.
He keeps cheerful, all things considered. He hasn't been feeling himself lately—the secretary of his fan club died of loneliness.
What a voice! Very handy in the event of fire or shipwreck ...
Not bad for thirty bob a week and first go at the left-overs.
He's my second favourite artiste—my favourite is anyone else
Last month he had the honour of being introduced to Her Majesty The Queen. Up till then he'd only seen her on a stamp so when he was presented he licked her face
He's just come back from a week's return engagement at the

## Your Distinguished Chairman

Empire, Leicester Square, where the manager reckons him as one of the best acts ever to entertain the queues

He'll be with us again next week so book now and ensure disappointment

He's shortly off to pantomime, playing the Prince in Dick In The Woods. Mind you, you can't imagine a Princess really fancying him. Not if she could get a good frog.

Someone said to me after last night's performance "I notice you always insult Mr --- when he's finished his act. I just want to say to you: keep up the good work."

He's a good friend—I often wheel him to the Post Office for his pension

See also General Exits (page 91) and Duet Exits (page 95)

## INTRODUCTIONS FOR LADIES

The Chairman should not over-elaborate the introductions for acts—a constant stream of saucy allusions and strings of alliteration become tedious. Where possible the introduction should be related to the song that follows, and a straight song should have a perfectly simple, brief and uncomplicated introduction. Sometimes it helps to remind the audience of an artiste's previous appearance, especially if a lengthy interval has elapsed, e.g. "We continue with Miss – – –, who you recall so delighted us earlier in the programme with (name of song). Now, however, we find her etc., etc."

The Chairman should bring his gavel down between the Christian name and surname of the artiste concerned: if this pattern is followed throughout the show it allows for exactness of timing by the band, the electrician and the stage-manager, not to mention the artiste herself.

Always prefix introdutions for ladies with the title "Miss", and pronounce "artiste" as "arteeste".

... the gorgeous, glamorous and gracious ...
... that pleasing personification of pulchritude ...
... that vital, vivacious and voluptuous vocaliste ...
... that pert and predatory parcel of pubescence ...
... that innocuous and ingenous incarnation of innocence ...
**(for French number)** the gay, gorgeous and Gallic ...
... that demure and dimpling damsel ...
... that blonde and blithely bonny balladeer ...
... that celebrated disseuse ...
... that wickedly witty and winsome ...
... that ever-popular serio-comique ...
... that captivating combination of comeliness and coquetry ...
... a young lady who never fails to delight, desport, nay, disarm ...
... a young lady whose dark beauty and steadfast virtue make my every waking moment a torture ...
Miss N will now exhibit herself upon this stage wearing *nothing* ... but a swimming costume ... (or leotard or whatever)
... for this number the management have decided that for its

correct rendition Miss N shall wear a costume of such startling *déshabillé* as has not been seen since Adam turned over a new leaf. But who will argue with such an artistic decision, when it reveals so many of the charms of your own Miss N!
... a young lady of many parts and all of them attractive ...
... a young lady whose talent is commensurate with her popularity, both of which are considerable ...
Miss N will be favouring us with a gay and jolly song as is her wont —and if Miss N won't, nobody will ...
... this young lady is new to us here ... in fact she is making her maiden appearance, in a manner of speaking ...
I exhort, nay, I entreat, nay, I *expect* you to stamp, whistle, applaud and huzza for Miss N!

(for **jilted girl number**) The jilted maiden is so often a figure of odium, obloquy and opprobrium. I ask you therefore to display the optimum kindness, consideration and compassion for Miss N ...

(for **sentimental number**) Miss N will now allow us into her inmost hopes, fears, expectations and regrets, as she sings for us (song title) ...

(for **nurse number**) She may be bad for your blood-pressure, boys, but she can give me a bed-bath any time. To tell us all about her adventures amidst the splints and the specimen bottles, is ...

(for **Dutch number**) Here, fetchingly arrayed in authentic Dutch costume of clogs, baggy trousers, waistcoat and Dutch ... headpiece, is ...

(for **French number**) Mademoiselle is known the length and breadth of the Champs-Elysées as Pattie de Faux Pas. She used to work as a *femme de chambre*—that's a girl who empties the ... ashtrays

(for **French Number**) Mlle N is of French extraction—her father was a dentist from Marseilles ...

(for **"grand dame" routine**) It is not for nothing that Mrs ——'s/ Lady ——'s welfare work among the troops has earned her the soubriquet of "The Private's Friend" ...

(for "*Don't Dilly Dally*") "We had to move away, 'cos the rent we couldn't pay" ... a rhyming couplet worthy of the Bard himself. Cognoscenti of the Music Hall will have recognized this quotation as being the first two lines of the first verse of Miss Marie Lloyd's most popular song: "*Don't Dilly Dally*"— number — on your song-sheets, to be rendered for us now in fine style by ...

(for "*Ain't It Nice?*") Our next item on the agenda features the delectable Miss N singing that plaintive aria "*Ain't It Nice*"? and I know you will agree with me when I say "ain't she nice?" ladies and gentlemen, as we welcome Miss N!

(for "*Why Am I Always the Bridesmaid?*") "Why am I always the bridesmaid?" weeps our next artiste. Can it be that life will pass by our Miss N? Is she for ever doomed to that solitary cup of cocoa at bedtime? Is her nightie for ever fated to remain around her ankles? Come, gentlemen, is there not one among you charitable enough to rescue Miss N from a fate worse than a fate worse than death? Let us now greet the sad and pathetic spectacle of Miss N! (weeping)

(for "*Daddy Wouldn't Buy Me A Bow-Wow*") "Daddy wouldn't buy me a bow-wow," sobs our next artiste, in number — on your song-sheets. A flinty-hearted parent indeed he must be to have refused *anything* of . . .

(**for any song with a request in the title, such as** "*Swing Me Higher, Obadiah*") Our next item is in the form of a *cri de coeur* . . . French! . . . (give title) pleads our forthcoming artiste, and who could deny that wearer of the face serene and bearer of the form divine, your own Miss N!

(for "*Has Anybody Seen My Tiddler?*") "Has anybody seen my tiddler?" squeals our next artiste—as nasty a little girl as ever disgraced herself on the front-parlour carpet. And in front of the vicar, too. *Has* anybody seen her tiddler? Does anybody care? However, I suppose we shall have to hear about it in grim and grisly detail from Miss N!

(**for shy little girl number**) Little Miss N is very shy, ladies and gentlemen, so she will need all your encouragement and indulgence, even though she is in fact the winner of this year's National Talent Competition for the Daughters of Deserving Spinsters . . .

(**for train number**) . . . our own Sweetheart of the Sidings . . .

(for "*When I Take My Morning Promenade*") Once again we welcome back to the podium Miss N, who this time will regale us with details of her pre-prandial perambulatory peregrinations . . . yes, it's the ever-popular "*When I Take My Morning Promenade*"— number — on your song-sheets. Here then, tastefully arrayed in some of the less well-known items from the (local) Theatre's wardrobe (or hire firm) is Miss N!

(**for song and dance**) A young lady whose terpsichorean exhibitions

## Your Distinguished Chairman

no less than her vocal expertise have long made her a firm favourite here . . .

Here's a young lady we haven't seen for some time, and personally I'm delighted to see her back . . . her front's not bad, either . . .

Which brings us to the first solo lady to grace our bill this evening; and Bill himself will be particularly pleased when I tell you that it is none other than . . .

**or** Now we come to a young lady who has not graced our bill for far too long an interval, and Bill's getting pretty cheesed off about it . . .

Miss N used to be known as the Toast of Tooley Street (or local) . . . in fact the last Duke to drink champagne from her slipper succumbed shortly afterwards to a bad attack of athlete's gullet . . .

Miss N will now display her art (glare at man in front row) . . . her ar*t* . . . in a sweet little number . . .

Miss N will now present the cutest little ditty . . . (glare at man in front row) . . . *Ditty* . . .

Miss N has the whitest pair of—shoulders east of the Grand Union Canal (or local)

**(for star spot)** Now we come to the climax of our entertainment this evening with the welcome appearance (or reappearance) of Miss N, and I am reliably informed that Miss N is no slouch when it comes to climaxes . . .

Miss N is always very popular here, I know, so I want a big hand on her opening if you please . . .

**(For a ballad)** To be sung effectively and affectingly by

This lovely lady is much sought after and, I am told, much yearned after

**(For 'virgin' number)** This item tells of the adventures of a young maiden— a virgin! One such will now be impersonated by . . .

**(For** *"I'll Make A Man Of You"*) We continue with number X on your song-sheets, "*I'll Make A Man Of You*", a song made famous by the surgical registrar of (local) hospital . . . there will be no blood letting tonight, however, but gentlemen I can assure you that you will be now well and truly operated upon by Miss – – –!

Miss – – – will be arrayed in a somewhat revealing costume, but try not to get over-excited, gentlemen. Keep yourselves firmly in hand, if you please

A veritable feast for the eye and ear

(For *"Who Were You With Last Night?"*) "Who were you with last night?" queries our next artiste accusatorially. So, married gentlemen, if you fancy a flighty philandering flutter beware the eagle eye of Miss – – –

Here she is with her death-defying stunt

Last time this attractive young lady was here she made a considerable impression on the male members of the audience, if you'll pardon the expression

Small but beautifully formed, it's the dinky little Miss – – –

It's the bewitching and bounteously buxom

Pure Brass of the Halls

Miss – – – will now give her celebrated male impersonation, correct down to the smallest detail, or so I am informed

The art of Bel Canto singing will now be demonstrated in all its glory by . . .

(For buxom lady in revealing costume) Here she is, in what can only be described as the flesh

Here she is, tastefully arrayed in blush pink and three/four time

And now for a most attractive lady with whom I've had the pleasure of performing on many occasions . . . no please, I mean she's a marvellous turn . . . on the *stage*. . .

(For *"Oh! Oh! Antonio"*) Our poor Miss – – – has been crossed in love. . . yes, she's been done wrong . . . and by an Italian ice-cream man! What a cad! Still, it's her own fault—she never could resist a king-sized cornet . . . no, please, don't take the pistachio, but instead let us commiserate with the betrayed, the benighted, the bereft Miss – – –!

Our own divine and delicious diva

Miss – – – needs no encomiums from me, so secure is her hold upon our affections

Not for nothing is Miss – – – known as the past-mistress of the significant gesture

When I came out to start the show Miss – – – hadn't arrived, but I'm sure that when I raise my knocker she'll come a-running . . . that usually does the trick

See also General Introductions (page 84) and Duet Introductions (page 94)

# EXITS FOR WOMEN

As with the introductions, the Chairman should not overdo his exit remarks—nothing is more boring than the Chairman who insists on doing a full patter routine between each item. Also he should endeavour not to intrude into the effect of a performance: just a quick one-liner if it has been a comic turn, or for a straight number "Thank you, Miss N, that was quite charming," is sufficient.

If an act has not been done well never, never make a derogatory remark. Just smile and say "Thank you Mr/Mrs ---. Well done. And now"—looking as though you are enjoying a duff turn is one of the hardest tasks the chairman faces!

She's very good to her mother—she never goes home . . .
Miss N can always be relied upon to scintillate . . . in fact she has been known to sin till nine
She's always so effervescent. In fact I never knew a time when she effer vasn't
I once had a crush on her but she threw me off
Miss N's figure is entirely supported by voluntary contributions
I've known her for many years—we have a lot in common. Actually it's Clapham Common we have a lot in . . .
She's a very athletic girl, you know—very fleet-footed. Loves running after sailors
We'll be seeing more of Miss N later on . . . in a manner of speaking . . .
Miss N has recently been immortalized by a famous artist on canvas . . . well, it makes a change from the floor
Wasn't that a lovely dress . . . I wonder who shot the couch?
Miss N appears by kind permission of the Chief Wardress of (local hostel)
Miss N is a lady celebrated in many fields, especially the one behind the Fire Station.
Hasn't Miss N a lovely voice? Mind you, look where it's been . . .
Miss N goes out with the boys by the score—though not all of them do
Miss N has a vast and enormous repertoire of Music Hall songs, learned at her mother's knee and other low joints
**(after rustic number)** There's nothing Miss N likes better than a

tramp in the woods . . .

(after "*Swing Me Higher Obadiah*") Love in a swing—how romantic . . . mind you, love in a hammock needs perseverance as well

(after "*Daddy Wouldn't Buy Me A Bow-Wow*" **when cat prop is used**) I am asked to inform any members of the RSPCA who may be present that the cat used by Miss N during that item was in fact . . . stuffed (look hard at audience)

(after **Irish number**) You'd never think to look at her that when she was a girl back in Ireland she used to dig for peat. Pete was her brother—he was always falling in the bog

(after "*Ta Ra Ra Boom De Ay*") I loved her ta-ra-ra and her boom-de-ay is second to none, or so I'm told . . .

(after "*Has Anybody Seen My Tiddler?*") There's nobody's tiddler I'd rather pinch less, personally

(after **French number**) Miss N acquired her French accent from a Johnny Onion man deal in Deal, which is why it's so strong . . . at least from where I'm sitting . . .

(after **French number**) Mlle N can accept a limited number of pupils for private French lessons . . .

(**After a number which finishes with the splits**) Ouch—that ending always makes me wince . . . I'm so glad when they get up still smiling

Miss --- told me earlier that she has just got engaged to an Irishman. "Oh, really?" I said. "No," she said, "O'Reilly".

Miss --- is very much a music lover though I understand she can do it in the quiet

What a woman! Even her dandruff is sexy

Every time I see her the water on my knee bubbles

She's very well reared . . . oh, you noticed, did you?

(**After an act in which a girl goes amongst the audience**) There's a girl who always makes her presence felt . . . yes, guaranteed to bring a tear to the eye and a lump to the trousers

Miss --- will delight us again with her ditties later on

She's a game girl—used to be married to a trapeze artiste, but she caught him in the act

Wasn't that a lovely dress? Mind you, I've had an interest in women's clothes for the past twenty years—on and off

(**After storming ballad which finishes on high note**) There she goes, taking her top B flat with her

(**After bosomy girl**) Thank you for that trip down mammary —memory lane

.

## Your Distinguished Chairman

Her uplift has led to many a downfall

Miss ––– was wearing her barbed wire dress. It protects the property without obstructing the view OR her hand grenade dress. Pull out one pin and it's every man for himself.

**(After railway number)** There's a young lady worth taking a sleeper from (local) to (local) for

**(After 'horsey' number)** She loves riding. Steeplechase—point to point—but I'm told she's particularly good on the flat

**(If Chairman has been vamped during a number)** I was nearly carried away then, which I'm told is not a pretty sight. Yes, I really had to keep a grip on myself

Miss ––– is a good girl and you can't keep a good girl down. Though I'm told it can be fun trying

**(After energetic number)** Well done. Go and put your feet up, dear—I'll be in to give you a rub down in the interval.

**(After a sexy number)** Phew! I wish it was the interval (Put finger in collar)

**(After girl with revealing dress)** I've seen nothing like it since I was weaned... I feel like a milk stout now, I don't know why

Every time I see Miss ––– I reach for my Iron Jelloids OR Phyllosan

**(After 'tart' number)** Miss N is now accepting bookings for the summer season

See also General Exits (page 91) and Duet Exits (page 95)

## GENERAL INTRODUCTIONS

These introductions can be used either for a man or for a woman; slight alterations here and there may make them suitable for many different kinds of act. I do not suggest that any of the gags in this book should be delivered exactly as printed—they should be tailored to fit the erstwhile Chairman's own personality and mode of speech. If you find that a joke does not raise a laugh, then change it and try something else. If a series of Music Halls is to be presented, don't put all the plums into the first programme: save some for later productions.

Some Chairmen introduce an artiste with a string of alliteratives, repeat them and then ask the audience to say them. This course of action is not advised, for the simple reason that it is a bore. Alliteration should be sparingly used: once at the opening of the show, once perhaps at the close, and not more than two or three times during the programme proper. Don't ask for a "warm welcome" on every single introduction, and avoid like the plague that dreadful cliché "put your hands together, please, for ..."

An audience should be coaxed into responding, not browbeaten. It usually takes a little time for a house to warm up—sometimes not until after the first interval, when everyone has had a drink or two. On the other hand, a noisy and/or inattentive audience should be worked on and brought to heel—so often Chairmen lose heart with an unruly audience and finish up playing to the front two or three rows only. Meeting trouble and overcoming it is the great challenge of the Chair—and how exciting and satisfying it is to win!

... and may I say that this act is very rarely seen at this price range
... this item, I can assure you, brings a tear in the eye, a lump in the throat, and a pain in the neck ...
... we shall now witness a display of a lady/gentleman—I use the word in the loosest possible sense—which only goes to confirm the generally held opinion that this country is going to the dogs
**(for straight opera spot)** And now a treat indeed for lovers of the vocal art ...
**(for specialities or unusual items)** I feel I should point out that this

act is not only extremely difficult for the executant but is also fraught with mortal danger for the front three rows of the stalls...

**(for cod sad number)** We now present what must be one of the most moving and affecting ballads in our music heritage...

**or** If you have tears, prepare to shed them now. Glasses down, eyes front and hankies at the ready, as we present that pathetic and pusillanimous plaint...

**or** Prepare now for an assault on the tender emotions as Mr/Miss N gives us that lilting if lachrymose lay...

**(where there is no balcony)** In response now to a request from the balcony, we present before your very glassy eyes...

Here now is an artiste who has long held an exalted place in your esteem and affections, and rightly so...

**(for coster number)** Here now is our own Pearly King/Queen. He/she comes all the way from Surrey...

This being the first Monday of the week, Mr/Miss N will oblige with...

... the ineffable, the insouciant, the irrepressible...

A young lady/gentleman possessed of a superabundance of that indefinable quality—charm...

Mr/Miss N will once again display his/her art...

Mr/Miss N is an artiste well known in concentric circles...

And so, without further ado, which I know will be a big disappointment to all his/her many fans...

It gives me great pleasure—not that my private life is any concern of yours...

Our next act needs no introduction. He hasn't turned up... so let us proceed with...

I ask now for a thundering round of indifference for...

It gives me very distant pleasure to introduce...

It gives me far-flung pleasure to introduce...

This aria will be sung in b flat or nearest offer...

Now, we present not three artistes, not two artistes, but one artiste —but that one artiste is more than sufficient when I tell you that it is none other than N!

And now, last and by all means least...

Here now is an auld acquaintance I would much rather have forgot... however, the management having gritted its teeth, turned its face to the wall and girded up its loins—if you'll pardon the expression—I will simply present to you...

Our next song takes the form of a cautionary tale . . .

**(for Scottish number)** Mr/Miss N is Scottish, not so much by birth as by absorption. He/she comes not from the Highlands but from the Lowlands—actually he/she comes from Limehouse (or local) and you can't get much lower than that . . .

**(when soloist is making a second appearance totally different from the first)** In this item Mr/Miss N executes a complete *volte face* . . . which as you probably know is only allowed at private performances **or** on (give day of the week)

This act is performed entirely in three dimensions . . .

Here now, *en route* for the Temperance Halls of Deptford and all points east (or local) . . . is N

For this next item, I know you will be acutely attentive, nay, avidly agog, nay—absolutely agape, as I introduce N!

Here now, *en route* for a tour of the Surrey Commercial Docks . . . (or local)

. . . we proudly present a leading luminary of the Salvation Army Citadel, Wapping Flats . . . (or local)

**(for song and dance)** During this item, Mr/Miss N will not only sing, but will also trip a tetrain of terpsichorean of *tours de jeté*! . . . Dancing . . .

**(for any solo instrumental act)** Mr/Miss N will now delight us by playing his/her very own guitar with his/her very own fingers . . .

**(for cod sad recitation)** . . . a sadly sanguine and sentimental saga as will cause the eyes of even the most mundane to moisten . . . as presented to us now by the Henry Irving/Sarah Bernhardt of (local) . . .

**(for nostalgic number)** What reveries, what reminiscences, what recollections of romance are conjured up for us by the title of our next song . . .

It is with pride, a stiff upper lip and fallen arches that I announce . . .

I now redeem a pledge made earlier in the evening—yes, once again it is time to greet the one and only Mr /Miss N, who will delight us with . . .

**(for fast number)** To be rendered now in spirited, if not spirit*ous* style by . . .

Ever-straining after novelties to divert you, the management is enrup—enraptured to bring to your attention . . .

Mr/Miss N now gives us a further taste of his/her quality with . . .

## Your Distinguished Chairman

It gives me peculiar pleasure to introduce our next artiste—not that he/she is in any way peculiar... I have to be careful what I say he's a devil with his handbag/she's a dead shot with that pipe —but because it is none other than...

**(for male impersonation)** Miss N now hides her undoubted femininity beneath a suit of male attire in order to impersonate the celebrated "*Burlington Bertie* . . ." **(for female impersonation alter as appropriate)**

Now we come to an artiste whose services the management has been endeavouring to avoid for some considerable length of time...

Your own, your *very* own...

Your own, and you can keep him/her...

Our next artiste is in great demand—in fact only recently she/he completed a split week at the Hippodrome Land's End and the Coliseum John o' Groats...

Mr/Miss N comes to us direct from a prestigious engagement at O'Grady's Kosher Curry House in the Mile End Road/Cohen's Chinese Beergarden (or local)

**(after announcing a song with a French title)** For those of you without the benefit of a classical (pronounced "clar-sical") education allow me to tell you that this, freely translated, means...

**or** those of you who speak French will have gathered from my impeccable Marseilles accent that this means...

**(after announcing suggestive song title)** I shall immediately stifle all those beige-coloured jokes which spring to mind—if you've got a mind like mine, that is, and shall simply announce: Mr/Miss N!

**(for autobiographical number)** Once again Mr/Miss N lurches into view, this time with a non-stop catalogue of his/her misdoings which would bring a blush to the cheek of Genghis Khan himself...

**(after announcing unusual, suggestive or puzzling song title)** However, all will be revealed—in a manner of speaking—by...

We now feature (song title) a song made famous by (give original singer's name) and here dispatched into oblivion by our own...

**(having announced a song title which is cockney or heavily regional such as "***Mrs 'Enery 'awkins***")**... if you'll forgive the lapse into the vehicular...

**(for "***Mother's Advice***" or "***The Gypsy Warned Me***" or similar**

**number)** What with skirts rising to fully two inches above the ankles and with young men discarding their spats all over the Home Counties, it would seem that our old-established moral codes are rapidly evaporating. However . . .

This is where Mr/Miss N really comes into his/her own. Well, no-one else will give him/her one . . .

Now we come to our grand scena of Songs of London (or whatever) numbers — to — on your song-sheets, and featuring (most of) the *entire* company!

Which brings us reluctantly but inevitably to our last and final item. This is yet another grand, spectacular scena—numbers — to — on your song-sheets, and featuring the *entire* company!

**(For any number with a suggestive title such as** "*Don't Have Any More, Missus Moore*" or "*John Willie, Come On*") I'm not sure what it was that Missus Moore had a surfeit of OR that John Willie has been up to, but I am sure that we can rely upon the good taste and discretion of

**(For omnibus number)** I tried to go riding on a bus last week but the horse wouldn't go up the stairs

To give us a taste of his/her quality

The curtain will shortly rise, very much against its better judgement, to display an artiste with a fine record—Enrico Caruso singing "On With The Motley"

Here now to get us off to a limping start is

So let's have a nice big raspb—round of applause—for

And now: it's lead balloon time!

Here is the one and only (thank God!)

Into each life some rain must fall, only in this instance it's our next act

And so I am underwhelmed to introduce

**(For skivvy or working-class performance)** Here then to give us a glimpse into life amongst the lower orders—something I'm sure none of us knows much about

For the next act we're really scraping the top of the barrel

It's a long time since we had a really good singer/comedian on the programme, and tonight—is no exception

Here now, snatched from the jaws of the Albert Hall

A really fine and popular artiste follows next; one of the most splendid and versatile and charming artistes I've ever had the pleasure to introduce! It is, of course, (look at notes and then say name in tones of stupefied horror). Who wrote this rubbish?

We now present a great threat—(look at notes again)—*treat*
Now I'd like to prevent—present
Our next artiste needs no introduction—he/she just needs an act
**(For Continental number)** Here now with a whiff of the Continent and more than a touch of garlic for the front three rows
You've heard the saying "this act needs no introduction"? Well, I can tell you this next act needs all the introduction it can get
Now the moment no-one's been waiting for; not only one of the country's finest Music Hall artistes but also the man who wrote this introduction
(Start reading heavily eulogistic introduction, getting slower and more laboured. Then look into the wings and say:) Sorry, I can't read your writing
And now on behalf of the management—and believe me, I'd like to be half of the management
This song will now be perpetrated by
What can be said about this next act in front of a mixed/family audience? Not a lot
**(For riding number)** Here then, cantering into view all bright-eyed and rosy-cheeked is Mr/Miss Mucking Out of 1882, known and loved by us all as
This song will be performed almost entirely from memory ... (can also be used for an exit if the performer has dried very noticeably)
Listen carefully to every subtle nuance ... that's a French word ... some of the artiste's gestures will be French as well
Here he is, the inimitable, the incomparable, the indefatigable, the absolutely indispensable
Here is a request from (read out lengthy list of names which can include notables in the audience) and all at 27 Gasworks Parade ... basement flat
This lovely old ballad will now be rendered to advantage by
For a straight ballad give names of lyricist and composer
This aria will be sung in B flat. Just give him a B, maestro, he'll flatten it himself
We usually have an interval about this time, only tonight it's called Mr/Miss ---
We continue with an artiste who is rapidly becoming an institution—some people say that's where it belongs
I won't say much about this next act—I'm trying to keep the show clean

We continue with a song made famous by Mr Harry Champion (or whoever) and now rendered into oblivion by

This next artiste will not only sparkle but will positively coruscate

We all know Mr/Miss --- of old—he/she has in our previous Music Halls so often been tried, tested, and found wanting

At this point we were to have an old Norwegian (or local) drinking song, sung by an old Norwegian drunk, but the closest we can manage is

He's/she's got more talent in his/her whole body than in the rest of his/her little finger ... that can't be right ...

Here now, fortified by the rites of the Church

Here now, primed with the finest Turkish chablis that money can buy

Always delighted to see our next artiste—we're related through drink

He's/she's only got one aim in life—pity he/she missed

Whenever I feel I need some exercise I just listen to N. sing and let my flesh creep

Now, good news for N's fans—they're a lovely old couple

N can sing like a mermaid/can do the splits

His/her last engagement was entertaining the troops in Lucknow—one at a time

(After strenous act) I don't know how he/she does it for the money ... but then I don't think he/she ever does it for the money

**(For naval number)** It must be wonderful being in the Navy—all those rowlocks and bollards and things

(If someone in the audience leaves during an introduction) Oh, don't you like Mr/Miss N?

See also Introductions for Ladies (page 76), Introductions for Gentlemen (page 66) and Duet Introductions (page 94).

## GENERAL EXITS

These are "back announcements" applicable, as with the section on General Introductions, either to men or to women, and also to various types of act. Sometimes a suitable exit remark can be made by incorporating the name of the artiste, i.e. I once introduced an artiste by the name of Gordon Pole. After his act—a comedy one, of course—I was able to say, "Thank you, Mr Pole. We'll be up later ..." This was a good laugh—a sympathetic and affectionate one, which is important. Naturally I had Gordon Pole's permission to use his name in vain. But again I stress that it is not necessary to try and top every act with a joke—just a simple "Thank you" will suffice in many instances.

He's/she's a remarkable chap/girl ... and you should hear some of the remarks ...
He/she comes from Wimbledon—and not so much of the Common, if you please ...
His/her voice is not so much trained as shunted ...
His/her voice as you could tell is not exactly trained ... in fact, it's not even housebroken ...
There's a song Stephen never Fostered ...
There's nothing like a good song, and I'm sure we all agree that that was nothing like a good song ...
Thank you, Mr/Miss N, and good luck with your forthcoming recital at the Albert—Memorial
Thank you and good luck with your forthcoming tour of the Hampton Court Maze
**(after comic number)** Thank you, Mr/Miss N, and a safe journey back to (local lunatic asylum district)
The magic lantern rights for that song have just been sold for the record sum of 2s 4d
I haven't laughed so much since my Army medical ...
I'm sure that act will be remembered long after it is forgotten ...
That is an artiste who should go a long way ... China, for instance ...
**(after naval number)** I've always had a hankering for life at sea ... all those rowlocks and bollards ...

I am not easily moved . . . but during that item, I very nearly went . . .

**(after conjuring act)** I understand that the Professor was instructed in the arcane mysteries of his art by the legendary Chinese sorcerer Wun Hung Lo . . . **(this can also be used after a juggling act, suitably amended)**

**(after glamorous drag act)** So different from the home life of our own dear Queen . . .

**(after accordion act)** I bet he's/she's glad to get that off his/her chest . . .

**(after navy number)** Thank God for the Army . . .

**(after army number)** Thank God for the Navy . . .

**(after saucy number)** Mr/Miss N is also a lay preacher at the Mormon Tabernacle, Balls Pond Road (or local)

**(after seaside number)** Thank you, Mr/Miss N for that whiff of the briny, and from where I am more than a touch of carbolic/mother's ruin . . .

**(After black-face number)** Thank you, Mr/Miss --- and good luck with the Lifebuoy

**(After a saucy act)** Now available for children's parties and parish functions or any reasonably sheltered street corner

That act has been passed by the Lord Chamberlain and the number 23 bus

I hope he/she enjoyed his/her farewell appearance

Beautifully and stylishly performed as we have come to expect

I didn't book him/her

Worth his/her weight in Guinness

A legend in his/her own lunchtime

Well, that's got that over

He/she has the makings of a great failure

I knew him/her when he/she was alive

Wonderful for his/her age—he's/she's only 23

I'm sure we'd all agree he/she should go far

**(After an act which has gone awry)** Come tomorrow and see a rehearsed version of that act

In all my experience I've never seen anything like that before

Good's not the word

He/she used to be a tap dancer but he/she kept falling in the sink

Mr/Miss --- last performed that act for the inmates of Wormwood Scrubs (or local prison) so we apologize to any of you who have seen it before

*Your Distinguished Chairman* 93

That song reminds me of my youth ... I think he joined the Navy

**(After sweetly romantic number)** Pretty raunchy stuff, eh?

**(After wild 'tramp' or similar number)** Wasn't that kind of the vicar/vicar's wife to oblige?

**(After 'tumult' act)** The only thing that could follow that is the end of the world. We couldn't arrange that so let's have the next best thing: our internationally renowned *interval*! (Hooray!)

**(After comedy magic act)** Mr/Miss --- is of course a member of the *Outer* Magic Circle

(If someone returns to their seat after an act) Oh, you missed a treat—what a shame ... could you hear us out there? We could hear you in here

See also Exits for Gentlemen (page 72), Exits for Ladies (page 81) and Duet Exits (page 95).

# DUET INTRODUCTIONS AND EXITS

If possible, the Chairman should be incorporated into at least one of the items in the programme—he can be vamped, for instance, by one of the girls during "*I Was A Good Little Girl Till I Met You*". Or he can be interrupted by the cast with some "crossover" gags, or by a comic while trying to give a serious recitation.

## 1 Introductions

We now present that charming and romantic old song (song title), rendered for us now in charming and romantic style by two of our most popular young artistes: Miss N and Mr N!

**(for barber-shop quartet)** . . . to be sung for us now in baggy trousers and suffocatingly close harmony by the gentlemen of the company!

These two artistes need no introduction . . . they've already met . . .

Miss N will now unite artistically with Mr N in that lovely old ballad . . .

. . . that prodigal, provocative and preposterous pair . . .

We are honoured tonight by the appearance on our humble podium of two of Society's brightest luminaries, Dame Patti Cake and Lady Virginia Water!

We now present not one artiste, but two artistes, each of whom will appear upon these hallowed boards at one and the same time! **(if male and female)** Moreover, each of these two artistes is of either (look both ways, then whisper) gender! (If someone shouts out "Sex!" Say, "Who said that? . . . See me afterwards in my dressing-room, will you?") Ingenuity can surely go no further . . .

In this double act Miss N works on the day shift and Mr N works on a night shift, so this is the first time they've done it together, if you'll pardon the expression . . .

**(for three hander)** . . . as rendered for us now by the Three—Twins!

**(for Chairman to be interrupted)** I would like now to raise the tone of the concert by giving you the opening speech of *Henry V* by . . . er . . . by special request . . . "Oh, for a Muse of Fire . . ." (he gets no further)

Welcome now to the Zola brothers, Emile and Gorgon!

(**for cross talk patter double**) Now, ladies and gentlemen, we would like to present the kind of act which has rather gone out of fashion nowadays. We think this is rather a pity because we think there is still a lot of fun to be got out of this kind of act, and that is the old cross-talk comedy routine, with the straight man and the red-nosed comedian. We don't pretend that any of the jokes you are about to hear are in any way new . . . but should you recognize any of them, greet them as you would an old friend . . . with warmth and affection . . . laugh if you can, boo if you must, but don't just sit there—do something! Now, I'd like to start by giving you Mark Antony's speech over the body of Caesar in the Roman Forum. "Friends, Romans, Countrymen—lend me your ears . . . !" (he gets no further)

## 2 Exits

(**after act which has been introduced as "The Brothers Karamazov"**) Thank you, the Brothers Karamazov . . . they're called the Brothers Karamazov because they're always Russian (rushin') about . . .

(**after two men**) I am asked to tell you that Messrs N and M are just good friends . . .

(**after comedy act featuring wife and henpecked husband**) Thank you, Mr and Mrs N, and I'm sure we'd all like to extend our sympathy to Mr N . . .

(**after comedy double by two girls**) Thank you, ladies. That was the Misses N and M—Miss N was the pretty one and Miss M was the . . . other one

**or** Miss N was the one with the beautiful soprano voice and Miss M was the . . . other one

**or if both are blondes:** Thank you ladies. That was of course the misses N and M. Miss N was the blonde.

(**give names**) I don't know which is which but I'm sure they do.

# LATE LAUGHS AND NO LAUGHS

Late laughs are a Chairman's joy—it shows that his audience is thinking; no laughs are his sorrow, but inveighing against an audience for not laughing can be a very dangerous procedure. For OAP audiences, the very effort of laughing and applauding is too tiring, which is why they show very little response although they will very likely have thoroughly enjoyed themselves. It is advisable for any clever, satirical or witty cracks to be omitted for OAP matinées, since they will almost certainly fall on stony ground, so offer 'story' jokes instead.

Sometimes the lack of a laugh can be turned to advantage, i.e. the Chairman can laugh heartily himself and then let his face crumple into tears—which will get a laugh and sympathy. It must also be remembered that the Chairman has to start on a completely cold audience; but he should not despair at not getting screams of mirth within two minutes of starting—nor should he berate his audience for not appreciating his gems of humour. The audience will gradually come to him and his earlier efforts at ingratiation will pay dividends. If, however, later on in the programme a joke repeatedly fails to get a laugh, it should be dropped rather than persevering with it and insulting the audience for failing to laugh. Also any joke which evokes a wince or intake of breath from the audience (either for being too near the knuckle or too unsympathetic) should immediately be cut.

An exit gag may prove, as the act for which it was intended progresses, to be unsuitable: don't risk antagonizing the audience—cut it and substitute something innocuous.

## 1 Late Laughs

Come along, come along, we've got a long show to get through...
Come along, come along—they shut at 10.30
Pass it along, will you?
**(when only one section of the audience laughs)** Here I'm doing comedy, there I'm doing tragedy...
You'll have to be quicker that that... I want to get through before the pills wear off OR The lights are fading my trousers

**(When man laughs late)** Have you just worked it out?... Well, put it back.

Don't laugh on your own—they'll think I'm working you with my foot

Are you a shareholder?

There's the man who had my transfusion

**(Unexpected big laugh)** I should have started with that

**(Unexpected laugh)** (check flies—turn and run hand along flies)

Take your time, it's a short show

**(When woman laughs late)** Are you being interfered with, madam? If not, why don't you move down here—I'm sure this gentleman would oblige...

**(When woman laughs raucously)** How can you look so clean and laugh so dirty?

That's right, dear. You lay 'em, I'll sell 'em.

She must have the seat with the broken spring.

(Look at pianist) Dear me, they're slow tonight. You can tell we're in the provinces (or local)

(Look at pianist) You won't be getting that last bus tonight, maestro... he wants to get home early—his mother-in-law's on heat

**(If one person only claps)** Don't clap on your own or someone might throw you a fish

If my old mother could see me now she'd be so ashamed—she thinks I'm in prison


## 2 No Laughs

Take notebook out of pocket, tear page out and throw it away

(look at pianist) Do you sometimes wish you'd never started something?

(Look at pianist) That went better first house... **(or at matinées)** That'll go better tonight (or) Do you know *Abide With Me*?

**(when raspberry is blown)** Are you expressing an opinion or do you have a cold?

**or** Can you make that noise with your mouth?

They don't write jokes like that any more... thank God...

**(laughs from Chairman only)** Let us pray... (bow head)

So this is where the good gags come when they die...

Have gavel—will travel...

I did hope we were going to be friendly ...
Please yourselves ...
All right, let's spend a nice quiet evening together ...
It may not be funny, but by the lord Harry—it's British!
I'm going to remember every last damn one of you ...
I don't have to do this for a living you know—I could always starve **or** I've got two Chincillas on heat.
What do you want at these prices—wit?
You're not really sure, are you ...?
I've been telling that joke for years and that's the best it's gone.
Sex, anyone?
Ah, you're a grand bunch of seats.
(suck thumb and walk to chair crying)
(look off) That's not an audience, it's a posse.
(look off) Is the car running?
Pick out the ones you like—I don't mind.
I must get a better brand of cracker.
That was my best joke. From now on it's all downhill.
That was like a joke ... not much like one I agree.
You try and get your money back.
(look off) Is the curtain up?
Are you sure Dan Leno started like this?
Do you think my style of humour will ever come back?

# SCENERY PATTER

The principal point of this section is to provide patter to cover any scene changes. It may be thought that not much has been allowed; again it is reiterated that the Chairman can very easily become sadly long-winded if he is not acutely aware of the danger. By the time the previous act has taken its calls, the Chairman has made his exit remark, announced the change of scenery and the details of the act or sketch to follow there should have been enough time to build a set of bricks and mortar let alone position one or two flats and props.

For amateur companies, care must be taken not to upset the scenic designer and painters—they work far too hard for much too little glory to have the mickey taken out of them with impunity.

Sometimes a virtue can be made out of the lack of facilities, e.g. I was once chairing in a theatre which had no house-curtains or runners whatsoever, and all scene-changes, such as there were, had to be effected in sight of the audience. On introducing the sketch, therefore, which required an interior set, I announced a complete change of scene, walked to the wings and extended my hand. A naked and obviously female arm came out carrying a hat-stand: I took it and placed it centre, looking off lasciviously. The hat-stand was placed U.C.—and there was our interior set.

**(for empty stage)** The scene, as must be obvious even to the meanest intelligence, represents . . .
Here, then, in a heavily scented boudoir redolent with the sensuous perfumes of the Berwick Street Market (or local) and with passion beckoning from every low satin pouffe, is . . .
At this point the (local) Theatre surpasses itself with a scene-change of such sublime symmetry and sesquipedalian superficies as can only be regarded as a thaumaturgic cynosure . . . translations are available after the performance . . .
The scene will change to one of stark simplicity in sharp contradistinction to our more usual elaborate settings and rich appointments . . .
**(for theatrical audiences only)** The scenery for this item was rather

unfairly purloined by a resourceful management from the late Mr William MacCready during one of his longer pauses...

The scenery for this item was purchased by a resourceful management from a sale of effects of the late Dowager Marchioness of Budleigh Salterton (or local) who will be so greatly missed by all ranks of the 23rd Lancers... gad, she was game...

When the great house-curtains divide you will see before your astonished and befuddled gaze a staggering assortment of tat cunningly arranged to represent...

The great house-curtains now close to allow our army of scene-shifters (poor old Gladys) to change the setting in the twinkling of an eye into a tastefully arranged empty space...

The scene changes in a flash to what can only be described as the euphuistic epitome of eclectic extravagance... you'll be able to see (name of local notable)'s parlour sofa for a start...

**(for French scene)** The scene is intended to conjure up for you the famous Rue de Postcard which lies in the shadow of the Eiffel Tower, the well-known Gallic symbol.

For the furniture used during that item we are indebted to Messrs Alf Ganker and Sons, stall number 4, (local) open market...

**(for rustic scene)** It is said that only God can make a tree. That may be true, but we here at the (local) Theatre can get pretty close... behold! (Tabs open)

Before your very glassy eyes will be the finest settings our overdraft will allow.

As you can see, every expense has been spared.

The decor kindly supplied by Messrs Bury and Burnham, funeral directors and embalming while you wait.

# HECKLE-STOPPERS

Heckle-stoppers are the very stuff of Music Hall—the more heckles the Chairman receives and the better he deals with them, then the greater will be his authority over the house and the greater his success. He must be careful, however, not to antagonize both the heckler or the audience. He must not be too cruel at first, otherwise he will stifle any further attempts to "have a go" from the audience. Alternatively, as happened to a friend of mine, he may receive a punch on the nose! Keep the squelches mild at first, getting more and more biting—especially if it is the same man or woman interrupting.

It can be unfortunate if the heckler takes offence, for he can then simply take refuge in abuse, spoiling the genial atmosphere. He may have his girl-friend with him, or a party of office pals, and he won't be best pleased to be made a fool of when he feels he is just helping the fun along. In such a case it is better to ignore him—as is the case with a quiet heckler, for it is no use giving the wittiest riposte in the world if the audience has not heard the heckle. One useful trick is to ask the heckler to repeat his remark. If he does so the audience will fall deadly quiet and ninety-nine times out of a hundred there will be no laughter whatsoever—the moment has passed. This leaves the field open to you to say cuttingly, "Do you know any jokes . . .?" But more often than not when you ask for a heckle to be repeated the perpetrator will lose his bottle and decline your invitation, enabling you to say "*Windy*!!!" One rather cruel trick I use occasionally is when you half-hear, and the audience half-hears, a heckle in a broad local accent; this can simply be answered by responding with an incomprehensible garble in what sounds like the heckler. Taking the rise out of someone's acccent is perhaps naughty, but anyone trying to get the better of a Music Hall chairman must be prepared to be cut to pieces. Sometimes when I have been especially successful at squashing a heckler I try to ease the pain by saying "Don't ad lib with me, son—I'll destroy you . . ." Persistent hecklers are best ignored or they will take over the show; the problem being that you often don't know they are going to be persistent until it is too late. I can only say that experience teaches you which hecklers to respond to and which to ignore: a very broad rule of thumb is that the closer to the stage a heckler is the safer you are to let his comments go unheeded.

Lady hecklers are rare and difficult to deal with. Usually—and I hope this will not be construed as a sexist remark because it arises from over twenty years' experience in the field and is not intended in any way as a put-down—ladies only heckle when they are drunk, and drunks are the Chairman's curse. A drunk will be quite insensitive to the mood of an audience and unaware of how boring his or her constant heckling has become. Drunks must be dealt with firmly, and if necessary ejected at the next interval, or everybody's evening will be ruined. I don't believe in pussy-footing about this. If two or three people in the house of two or three hundred are wrecking the evening—throw 'em out. Fast. Then the disturbance is over and done with and everyone can sit back and relax and let the show continue undisturbed. I have on occasion simply brought the show to an unscheduled halt for this very purpose, and all Chairmen should be ready to be firm and decisive on this point. Finally, don't be afraid to let a heckler get the better of you from time to time. If a heckle brings the house down and you can't think of a 'topper' don't spoil the fun as I have seen some Chairmen do by throwing a standard rejoinder at him. Laugh heartily to show what a fine sport you are and say something good-natured like "Can you come again tomorrow?" or "I am enjoying myself tonight".

## 1 Men

**(to incoherent shout from man)** Yes, madam? **(or from woman)** Yes, sir?
Hello, sir—you don't mind me calling you "sir", do you? . . . it's just in fun . . .
He's suffering from bottle fatigue . . .
Who wears your clean shirts?
Who shines your suits?
I like the way your teeth are parted in the middle . . .
Please, why don't you move closer to the wall—that's plastered already . . .
The last time I saw a mouth like that there was a hook in it
You sound a little hoarse . . . or at least like part of a horse . . .
What a pity your mother never had children . . .

## Your Distinguished Chairman

Hello, liquor mortis has set in . . .
Remind me to come to your parents' wedding . . .
I think his Ovaltine is fermenting again . . .
Why don't you sit down and rest your talent?
Hello, there must be a full moon tonight
If you were a woman I'd punch you right on the nose
**(to persistent heckler)** If I'd known I was doing a double act I'd have asked for more money
Watch yourself, sir—I must warn you that I'm not only the Chairman, I'm also chucker-out . . . (half taking jacket off)
**(to noisy party which arrived late)** You came late—would you like to go early?
**(after unpleasant interruptions during previous act)** Our thanks to Mr/Miss (name of artiste) and no thanks at all to the feeble-minded/ill-mannered specimen sitting over there . . . (this usually gets a round of approving applause)
**(if there is constant talking from a person or party during an item)**
If you wish to talk may I suggest that you retire to the bar?
I'm sure you'd be more at home there . . .
No school tomorrow?
Watch it, son—I could be your father
Any more remarks and your wife and me are through. (*If this elicits the come-back "I'm not married" continue with "No, like your father before you. . ."*)
I think he was vaccinated with a gramophone needle
**(To shout of "Get 'em off!")** You couldn't afford it OR I bet you say that to all the boys . . .
If you don't keep quiet I'll bring the comic on again
Keep Britain tidy—get out
Don't you think I'm funny? I laughed when you came in
You'll be a great wit someday—you're half-way there already
Won't your mouth be pleased when your tongue gets tired
They're lovely at that age
The reason he's making such a nuisance of himself is that he's miffed at the management for not letting him take part in the show. He wanted to do his female impersonation act . . . but we couldn't find enough lipstick to go round his mouth.
Put your cap on—there's woodpeckers flying about
**(To hissing)** Are you letting the hair out of your head?
Go home—the lodger'll be wanting his trousers back
You remind me of my father's coachman

You're making a big mistake — like your father before you
Is that a shirt or do you keep pigeons?
Please — you're embarrassing your daughter
What colour was that suit?
I'm sorry I'm missed that — I was talking
Your tongue would like nice on my sideboard
Where I come from we bury our dead
I've never really believed in Darwin's theory but looking at you I'm not so sure
He's sharp as a tack — anyone got a hammer?
Why weren't you at rehearsals?
Please have your nervous breakdown somewhere else
It's people like you that turn people like me into agents
Go home — your cage'll be cleaned out by now
I've always said cousins shouldn't marry
**(To shout of "Make us laugh" or similar)** If I was wearing that suit I would
Yes, I remember when I had my first beer
You can tell he's from (*local*) by his accent
When you had your tonsils out they threw away the best part (*If this elicits the come-back "I haven't had them out!" continue with "that can be arranged . . ."*)
Have you noticed how often a closed mind goes with an open mouth?

## 2 Women

What's the matter — is your housemaid's knee acting up again?
What's the matter — did you have trouble parking your broom?
Hello, it's Miss Stomach Pump of 1883
She'd make a wonderful stranger
Now I remember you — ten years ago at the (local) Theatre . . . I remember the dress
Well, if it isn't Jeannie with the light brown teeth
I like the fur: when do you feed it?
**or** It does a lot for you — but then that's only fair . . . you did a lot for it
It'll all end in tears . . .
Oh, she must be a handful at home . . .
She looks like a million . . . or perhaps a little younger . . .
Pay no attention — it's my mother, she's been at the Bev again

You remind me of a beautiful Italian girl I used to know . . . must be all that spaghetti down your front . . .
It's a one-woman orgy!
Lassie, go home.
Mother! You should be outside parking the cars.

# SKETCHES

It is always fun if the Chairman himself can play the villain in the sketch—and every Music Hall programme should include one. I have in fact regularly included two sketches ("The Drunkard's Dilemma" and "The Wages of Sin", both by Andrew Sachs and edited by myself in *Three Melodramas*, published by Samuel French, 1970) which allow this, and which provide the audience with plenty of opportunities to boo the Chairman—opportunities which are always grasped with enthusiasm and, one hopes, affection.

Again, the introduction should not be drawn out too long. Once the audience knows that the sketch is coming, get on with it, otherwise there will be altogether too much talk in one chunk.

## 1 Introductions

This dramatic playlet will feature a company of legitimate artistes
—that makes a change . . .
The entire second half of our programme will be given over as advertised to our grand, spectacular, melodrama-extravaganza. This section of the programme is not for the squeamish, but those of you foolhardy enough to maintain an intelligent interest in the proceedings are asked to warn, encourage and abjure the *dramatis personae* where appropriate
. . . and presented for us by now: the Billericay Barnstormers! (or local) **or** the Thanet Thespians!
Here, then, in all its torrid torment and tempestuous tumescence —whatever that may mean—is . . .
We now present as advertised our dramatic interlude of high moral tone and salutary intent, entitled . . .
**(for two-handed sketch)** and rendered for us now by two of England's finest Thespians—Sir Herbert and Lady Beerbohm Bush!
Prepare now for your withers to be wrung—have you ever had your withers wrung, dear? . . . No, well, you need to be fit . . .
For those of a nervous disposition we would advise you during

# Your Distinguished Chairman 107

this item to avert your gaze or to take refuge beneath the seats and tables . . . who knows? The entertainment there may be far more interesting . . .

It is suggested that the hero, heroine and villain—if not played by the Chairman—should be introduced before the sketch starts with a suitable rhyming couplet for each. This will encourage the audience to react enthusiastically during the action, e.g.:

> "I ask you now to give a cheer,
> For Gwendoline, our heroine dear!"

Enter Gwendoline, who curtsies to the audience, blows a kiss to the Chairman, and exits. Similarly—only without the kiss—for the hero and the villain

We now present our traumatic—dramatic—sketch.

(**for Shaw's** "*Passion, Poison and Petrifaction*") We now proudly present a one-act play whose essential jollity and light-heartedness are reflected in its title: *Passion, Poison and Petrifaction*. The author, I'm sorry to say, is that scandalously left-wing music critic, Mr. Bernard Shaw, but I can assure you that we in this House do not embrace his principles, whilst we are happy to present his piece . . .

Try not to cry in your beer—it's weak enough as it is.

## 2 Sketch Closers

(**if Chairman has played villain**) I thought the chap who played the villain was jolly good, didn't you . . . ?

Ah, dear me . . . not a dry seat in the house . . .

Well, there's nothing like a good play, and I'm sure we would all agree that that was nothing like a good play

Just let that be a warning to you.

If a cast is not included in the programme, be sure to announce the cast members from the stage.

I am not easily moved . . . but during that sketch I very nearly went . . .

(**when interval follows immediately**) In order to enable you to ingest both the moral of the play and anything which may be on sale for ready cash in the bars, I now proudly present—the Interval!

Further suggestions for openers and closers are given in my four books of sketches (see preface to second edition)

# INTERVALS AND LOYAL TOAST

It is preferable to have only one interval, but if the bar sales are important financially, then two of no more than ten minutes each may be programmed.

Never say "And now for the act which closes our first half" or the wretched performer will have to battle against a large and thirsty section of the audience making for the bar. The interval is no place for a long spiel unless the Chairman cunningly says what he has to say (an announcement of a raffle, for instance) and *then* announces the interval.

**1 Before**

We can't afford a second interval so here is the first interval all over again!

The management now proudly presents the (first) *Interval*!

During the interval there will be a collection for the Music Hall Chairman's Benevolent Fund. Please give generously, as the wife says I need a new knocker. (Brandish gavel and bang, blowing out candle at the same time)

**or** the (local) Temperance Guild. Membership forms are available in the foyer, entrance fee sixpence or three bottle-tops.

**or** the Old Ladies Home, so if you have any old ladies . . .

The Maestro and I will now retire behind the arras, where we shall talk about you . . .

The festivity will resume in ten minutes, after which time I hope to find you refreshed and watered . . .

Everything on sale at the bar is of the very finest quality—even the water has been passed by the management

During the interval we ask you to make free use of the conveniences provided—alcoholic on your left and necessary on your right. Try not to confuse the Ladies and the Gentlemen's retiring-rooms . . . if you do it may be embarrassing, but think of the friends you'll make . . .

... to enable you to charge your glasses and to discharge your debts. During the interval drinks will be entirely free! However ... a nominal charge will be made for the use of the glasses ...

Everyone present here tonight is entitled to a free drink ... yes, a free drink with every thirty-bob packet of crisps ...

Drinks are available at prices to suit all pockets, especially those of the management

May I particularly recommend the Scotch whisky on sale in the bar? Every bottle on sale here is guaranteed aged for a minimum of 43 minutes in one of the finest bath-tubs in Glasgow ... come to think of it, one of the *only* bath-tubs in Glasgow ...

Well now, I think a swift half is in order after all that so I think we'd better have the (second) interval. Our large and well-trained staff is on hand to take your orders, and you can rest assured in the knowledge that if you don't get the drinks you order, someone else will

**(when interval follows sketch)** I think that after that we could all do with a spot of the stuff that cheers and inebriates, don't you? So let us repair to the bars, and reassemble here, in, shall we say, ten minutes? Thank you

**(after a very strong act)** "Follow that," as they say. And what could possibly follow that other than the first (or second) interval!

The first interval was so successful we thought we'd have another just like it.

The Maestro will now play us off with that great favourite—The Stiffening Movement from Rigor Mortis

## 2 After

(bang gavel) Did you enjoy the interval? The best part of the evening I always think ...

(after gags, bang gavel again) And *that* brings us to the third and final half of tonight's proceedings—yes, we always have three halves in a Music Hall—we like to give value for money

I trust I find us all suitably refreshed and relieved ...

Are you all enjoying yourselves? ... Why, what are you doing?

I regret that I must start the second half with something of a disappointment for you ... we were to have started the second half with the Dance of the Three Virgins ... unfortunately ... they've broken their contract

Ladies and gentlemen, I'd just like to say how gratified I am—

during the interval the management very kindly made me a presentation in recognition of my services. They presented me with a ten pound tin of baked beans ... I'd just like to say: I'm deeply moved

**(To someone late back to their seat)** I hope you haven't been writing on the walls again ... could you hear us out there? No? We could hear you in here

**(Reading a piece of paper)** I have an urgent message for the young couple who came from (*local*) in a horse and buggy ... where are you? Ah, over there—you came from (*local*) in a horse and buggy? The message is from the horse ... he says can he have his oats now—you can have yours later ...

Would the owner of horseless carriage licence number 12X9453JB427KBD52964H9032KL4 please move his vehicle as the number plate is blocking the road?

See Miscellaneous (page 120)


## 3 Loyal Toast

And now, we start the second half of the evening's agenda with a most important ceremony—the Loyal Toast. I will ask you all to rise and to join with me in drinking the health of our gracious Sovereign Lady ... all rise, if you please ... all rise ... please rise, sir, I know it's been a long time ... come on, now, all on your feet. Show respect to the Sovereign if not to me ... (If some people are reluctant to rise the Chairman can say, "Up!" "Up!" "Up!" This will be taken up by the rest of the audience—but beware old people and the disabled). Last one up's a Marxist ... very well, ladies and gentlemen—Her Great and Glorious Majesty—Queen Victoria! (*Drink*) God Bless Her! ... Do sit down—you look ridiculous ... damn cheek ...

Then can follow any Birthday and anniversary announcements, after which the Chairman bangs his gavel to signal the return to the programme proper, e.g. Enough of entertainment, now on with the show ... !

See Miscellaneous (page 120) and Fillers (page 114)

# CLOSERS FOR SHOWS

At the end of the show, which is generally a popular chorus featuring all the cast, the Chairman takes his bow and then extends a hand to the accompanists, who take their bow—also bowing to the Chairman. Assuming the show has been a roaring success, the Chairman must not take the edge off the highly-charged atmosphere by weak and/or unnecessarily protracted material. It is customary to offer a long list of thanks in amateur productions: if possible dispense with these entirely—it's all or none on these occasions, and perhaps none is best.

The show is all over bar the shouting, and the Chairman should not seize this moment to do a ten-minute solo spot—especially as he will probably have the cast lined up behind him with egg all over their faces. But whatever gags he does use, it is as well to remind the cast to laugh as though they are hearing them for the first time, otherwise it can look as though the entire company have it in for him for some backstage misdemeanour.

Speak sparingly and to the point—and get off. It is quite a good idea to have a final farewell chorus in which the Chairman can join—first having blown out his candle—so that the curtains come down on the complete cast and the ending of the show is clean. Or, where there is no house curtain and the cast file off singing, he can join on the end of the line and exit singing with them and waving his tankard. (Don't leave it out front—it might be stolen . . . !)

Rest assured, ladies and gentlemen, that by the assiduousness of your attention and the amplitude of your applause, you remain incontrovertibly and incontestably the finest Monday night audience we have had—*this week!* (All the cast can join in with "This week!")

But seriously you have been marvellous—you lot can come again—and if you've enjoyed it half as much as we have, then we've enjoyed it twice as much . . . or something . . . (Look puzzled)

Our next production will feature a complete change of programme—I'll even be changing some of my material . . . well, my socks, anyway . . .

(after a list of thank-you's) . . . and I'd like to thank my parents for having me . . .

And thank you for being such a wonderful audience, because without you out there we couldn't do it up here, if you'll pardon the expression . . .

Thank you for your support—I shall wear it always . . .

And we'd also like to thank N, without whose help this show would almost certainly have got on . . .

If you've enjoyed the show, please tell all your friends, and if you haven't—keep your traps shut

If you've enjoyed the show, please tell all your friends, and if you haven't—well, (blow raspberry) to the lot of you. (This is a big laugh if done quickly and with a smile)

Do be careful as you go home tonight, because statistics show that in the borough of (local) alone, one man is knocked down every fifteen minutes—and he's getting pretty fed up with it

I must go now: I've got to get back to Elmer's End . . . and he's a a very demanding lad . . . (alter to suit local place name)

**or** my mother-in-law's home on leave . . .

**or** my mother-in-law's out on parole . . . OR on heat

**or** if I'm not back by eleven the wife lets out my room . . .

Our next programme will feature a plethora of carefully selected and highly regarded artistes, including: Harry Sludge, with his wonderful soft-shoe and hard-sock routines

**or** that ever-popular Anglo-Jewish trampoline act, Morris Dancer and the Maypoles

**or** Moira Pules the underwater soprano

**or** the soprano extraordinary, Mr George Shorthouse

**or** Henry Ballcock, the Cornish Pisky, who comes to us flushed with success . . . from his record-breaking season at Looe

**or** Percy Piledriver playing gems from *"Merrie England"* on the linoleum

**or** Suicide Sam the Human Canonball—you don't often see an artiste of his calibre

**or** Roger Fudgeknuckle the whistling undertaker—he'll be here, engagements permitting

**or** Beryl, the educated warthog—always a very strong act

**or** Hack and Spit the Flemish comedians

**or** Lord Privy and his performing seal

**or** Guttapercha Gertie the clairvoyant contortionist. She can foresee her own end. She can bend over backwards and bring

## Your Distinguished Chairman

her head up right between her legs. She does some interesting things in her act as well.

**or** That renowned knife-throwing act—Los Ababananos and Doris

They'll be here, provided Doris has had the stitches out in time...

**or** Big Chief Running Waterworks and his Braves... that's a very colourful and exciting act with all those tomahawks and choppers waving about all over the stage...

**or** the shortest Indian fire-walker in the world—Sinjis Thing

And top of the bill will be the one and only Miss Marie Lloyd, who will be treating us to her latest success: "She Sits Among The Lettuces And Leaks". She will also be giving us the sequel: "She Sits Among the Cabbages And Peas".

And so from all of us up here to all of you out there, thanks once again, good night—and God bless! (Band plays intro. to final chorus)

It's been a real financial pleasure

Thank you, and before the collection...

Thanks for coming. Thanks even more for stopping

Thank you from the bottom of my cheque-book

Did you enjoy the show?... Would you come again?... Would you pay more money?

Our sincere thanks to N, without whose help it would all have been so much easier

Thanks for the use of the hall

You've been a lovely audience—and I'm hard to please

I'm ready for bed—anyone?

We'd love to stay, but we're already into injury time

Thank you for having me. And for those who haven't, please be patient

It isn't generally known but all the proceeds from tonight's performance will tomorrow morning be going directly to ... Barclay's Bank

I've got another show to do—next March

Sweet dreams—you meet a better class of people I always find

We'll never forget you. No matter how hard we try

I'd love to stay but at midnight I turn into a pumpkin

I've got a job at the livery stables... and my work's piling up

See Miscellaneous (page 120)

# FILLERS

Very often the Chairman will be asked to fill in between items to cover a difficult scene-change or costume change. Rather than tell jokes, which as I have said before should be left to the comics, I suggest that the Chairman use one of the following short routines. They are also useful in an emergency, such as the occasion when I had actually begun to announce the next artiste only to hear a loud whisper from the wings telling me "she's got a nose-bleed!"

(**With piece of paper**) I have here an urgent message for Mr Fred Sponge of Gasworks Parade ... Mr Sponge, are you with us? ... Over there? The message is from the (*local*) maternity hospital and says that you have just become the father of a bouncing baby boy! ... and would you please go home as your wife would like a few words with you ...

Here is a message for the young couple who came from (*local*) in a horse and buggy ... from (*local*) in a horse and buggy? Over there? The message is from the horse. He says "can he have his oats now? You can have yours later"!

Our musical director's wife has just given birth to a bouncing baby boy! Would the proud father please rise? (*The other musicians rise*)

(**To couple**) Is that the wife with you, sir? Oh, novelty night ... where are you from, may I ask? ... Oh, from (*local*)? I read in the paper only the other day that there was a survey done in (*local*) which showed that fifty per cent of the married women in (*local*) are unfaithful to their husbands! ... and the Archbishop of Canterbury wrote a letter to the other fifty per cent! And do you know what he said, dear? ... Didn't you get one?

This is a lovely part of the world, isn't it? And they were telling me just before the show about the famous Echoing Cave of (*local*). You must know it ... no? Oh, well, it seems that last summer a young man—a tourist from (*local rival town*)—was very anxious to visit this Echoing Cave. So out he went one Sunday, tramping for hours and hours across the moors; the afternoon was wearing on and he was beginning to think he should turn back when suddenly, rounding a crag, he saw this large cave entrance down in the valley. "That must be it!" he said to himself, and down he scrambled to the entrance, where he held his hands up and shouted (*in deep tones*) "Yoo-hooo!" Will you help me with this, gentlemen? Thanks ... so he held up his hands and he shouted (*in deep tones*) "Yoo-hooo!" And he was thrilled to hear the famous echo! Ladies—you're the echo. What did you hear! (*In high-pitched tones*) "Yoo-hooo!" Daft as brushes, the lot of you ... anyway, the young man decided to try again, so he walked a few yards into the cave and again went (deep) "Yoo-hoo!" And again he heard the echo—(*high tones*) "Yoo-hoo!" "Marvellous!" he thought, so he walked in even further, and for the third time he went (*deep*) "Yoo-hoo!" And for the third time he heard the echo (*deep*) "Yoo-hoo!" And ten seconds later he was knocked flat by the 6.15 from Paddington (*or whatever London terminus is appropriate*).

As we have some youngsters in I thought I'd tell you all a charming little story. Will you help me? ... Will you? Thank you so much—I've been up all day, it is a shame. Now, this story is about three little ducks called (*hold up one finger*) Quack, (*two fingers*) Quack-Quack, and (*three fingers*) Quack-Quack-Quack—oh, you are quick! Shall we try that again? Three little ducks called (*one finger*) Quack, (*two fingers*) Quack-Quack, and (*three fingers*) Quack-Quack-Quack. Splendid! These three little ducks lived in the country—as all good little ducks should—and one day they decided that they rather fancied some mushroom soup. So out into the fields went the three little ducks called (*one finger, two fingers*) and (*three fingers*) with a big basket. They filled it to the brim with mushrooms, took it home, made the soup and drank it to the last drop. And it was scrumptious! But in the middle of the night (*one finger*)—come along now, have you forgotten already? In the middle of the night (*one finger*) feel ill! Ahhhh ... so, (*two fingers*) said to (*three fingers*) "You'd better go for the doctor". And he did, and the doctor came and examined (*one finger*), and said "Oh, he'll be all right. He's just got a touch of indigestion. Give him these pills and he'll be perfectly all right by morning." But, by the time morning came (*one finger*) had died! Ahhhh ... Whereupon (*two fingers*) said to (*three fingers*) "I think that doctor must be a bit of a (*one finger*)!" Well done, thank you so much.

*Note:* The "well done, thank you so much" *is important to get the final laugh and to round the routine off*

Our box-office lady, Miss Helen Hunt, tells me that a wallet has been found containing rather a lot of money. So if any of you gentlemen have lost a wallet, you can go to Helen Hunt.

Because of the low-lying site of this building and our proximity to the river, I know some of you are worried about the dangers of flooding. May I reassure you that the management have installed—at ENORMOUS expense—a new flood-warning device. This takes the form of a flashing buoy ... so if you should see the buoy flashing ... furiously ... just move against the walls and give me a clear run for the door—I can't swim a stroke.

I wonder whether you'd indulge me for a few minutes? I've been handed what we in the profession call a fan letter ... I don't get many, so would you mind if I read it? (*Read letter*) "Dear Mr N, I am writing to say how sorry I am that I won't be able to see you at the (*local theatre*)." Ahhhh ... "I have been a devoted admirer of yours for years ... but the trouble is my husband simply won't let me out of the house, due to his sudden insatiable appetite for ... affection! It is terrible! It doesn't matter what I am doing, he just keeps on—"(*Turn letter over then turn back*) "—keeps on. Whether I am cooking or cleaning or ironing or dusting, he just wants to make love to me all the time! So I hope you will understand why I'll have to give your show a miss this time. Yours sincerely, Mrs So-and-so. P.S. Please excuse the wobbly writing ..." (*Give a double-take and then carry the letter back to the Chairman's table holding it gingerly by one corner*).

(*Hold hand flat with palm upwards*) We have someone very special watching the show this evening—someone I brought back from my last trip to Ireland. He is, of course, a little leprechaun ... isn't he sweet? Of course, being outside the Emerald Isle, like all leprechauns he is invisible but he's enjoying the show and told me he most particularly wanted to meet that young lady in the front ... (walk down to girl in audience) There she is, Mickey ... he likes you, my dear ... tickle him under the chin. Go on—tickle him under the chin ... (*the victim almost always does a tickling mime about six inches above Chairman's hand. Chairman then holds his other hand to indicate Micky is in fact about a foot high*) he's actually that tall but he enjoyed that!

You won't mind, will you, if I read a letter I've just been given? Because it's from my dear old Mum ... ahhhh ... well, you travel a lot in this business—the way I work you have to keep on the move—and I haven't heard from home for about six months so you won't mind if I read it now? Not as it's from my dear old Mum? Ahhhh ... She says, "Dear Son ..." Well, she would, because—she's my dear old Mum ... Ahhhh ... "You won't know the old place when you come home—we've moved! The new house is very nice but the washing machine isn't working properly." Ahhhh ... "The first time I tried it, I put in fourteen shirts, pulled the chain and I haven't seen them since. Your sister May—" Oh, my kid sister's had a baby! "Your sister May had a baby this morning, but I don't know if it's a boy or a girl so I don't know yet whether you're an aunt or an uncle." (*Look puzzled at pianist and mutter 'aunt or an uncle?' to yourself*) "Your Uncle Patrick—" Oh, dear—tragedy! Ahhhh ... "Your Uncle Patrick drowned last month—in a vat of whisky at the Dublin distillery where he was working. His mates tried to pull him out but he fought them off bravely. I went to the doctor's—" "Oh, she's been ill! My poor old Mum! Ahhh ... "I went to the doctor's yesterday. Your Dad came with me. The doctor put a little glass tube in my mouth and told me not to talk for sixty seconds. Your Dad offered to buy it from him!" (*Laughing— 'oh, I don't believe that'*) Your brother Charlie—" Oh, he does suffer—Charlie! Ahhh ... depression—he's a martyr to it. "Your brother Charlie's been depressed again. Last week he went and ... and ...." Her writing's terrible! Is that an I or an O? Oh, it's an I! Oh, thank goodness for that—I thought she said he'd shot himself ... "Nice weather this week, it only rained twice. Once for three days and once for four. It was so windy that one of the chickens laid the same egg three times. I've just had all my teeth taken out—" turn page over "—and a new fireplace put in. God bless you and keep you from your loving Mother. P.S. I was going to enclose a £5 note but I'd already stuck down the envelope." Isn't that nice to hear from the old mater ... ?

For my next experiment I would like the assistance of a young lady from the audience ... can I have a volunteer? ... thank you dear. And your name? Mary? Thank you so much for making a fool—for coming up. Now then, I want you to take this packet of sausages ... please examine them carefully and ensure that they are just ordinary everyday sausages—beef, of course. Everything is kosher in this show ... are you satisfied? Thank you. I will now ask you to shuffle the sausages ... that's right, mix them up well and truly and give them back to me ... I will now fan the sausages out and avert my gaze ... will you, Mary, take one of the sausages? Any one at random ... have you done that? Please show it to the audience ... you don't want to change your mind? Very well, now I want you to memorise that sausage ... have you done that? Good, now place it back in the pack ... take the sausages and give them a good shuffle ... that's it ... give them back to me and I will endeavour, through my psychic powers, to determine which is the sausage that you selected ... (*throwing them into the audience one at a time*) It's not that one, not that one, not that one—but that one, Mary, is your sausage! (*Give it to her and get her off-stage quickly!*)

*Note*: The sausages should be raw, making them floppy and sticky and quite obscene—your volunteer could also be given a tissue as she leaves the stage to wipe her hands. If any lady has had a birthday mentioned earlier in the programme she could be called up, otherwise I have found it as well to have a quiet word during the interval with any likely lady sitting at the front to ensure that you have a ready volunteer. Final word of warning: don't be surprised if the sausages are thrown back!

    King Solomon had ten thousand wives,
    He serenaded 'em daily;
    But what's the good of ten thousand wives,
    When you've only got one ukelele?

    Annie and Fanny were sisters,
    You'll see them walking about;
    Annie's the one with her teeth in,
    And Fanny's the one with them out.
    Though Annie's the one that I'll marry,
    I'm sure you'll think it quite fair;
    When I've tied the knot,
    With what little I've got,
    I'll see that they both get a share!

A list of turns "in our next programme" as given on page 112 can also make a handy filler.

## MISCELLANEOUS

During the course of a show the Chairman essays anywhere between fifty and seventy humorous remarks, so don't feel suicidal if they aren't all greeted with gales of mirth—if you score anything over fifty per cent you're doing well!

**(to party dressed in period costume)** I'd like to say a special "hello" to the party of refugees from Moss Bros ... no, you look splendid, really ... I'm quite jealous of that coat, sir ... and what a wonderful moustache over there ... (peer hard) ... oh, I beg your pardon, madam ...

I'd tell you more jokes but you'd only laugh ...

Ladies and gentlemen—Ladysmith has been relieved! ... (after cheers) ... his lordship is not available for comment

**(after big laugh and cheers on an old joke)** We love a joke we know ...

**(after old joke which gets a big laugh)** I do like an audience with a short memory ...

**(after joke where audience has joined in the tag)** All join in the chorus

I regret to say that during the interval I have had a complaint from a lady. She said to me, "Mr Chairman, during the show so far I've had to change my seat six times." "Why, madam?" I said. "Were you molested?" She said, "Yes—eventually!"

**(for a visit of civic dignitaries)** If I pull that chain—will you flush?

**or** There was a young lady of Wantage,
Of whom the Town Clerk took advantage;
Said the borough surveyor
"You'll have to pay 'er,
You've considerably altered her frontage!"
That wasn't you, sir, of course ...

**(look into tankard)** The bottom of this tankard is distinctly damp ...

**(when there is drinking in the auditorium take tankard and turn it upside down, showing ostentatiously that it is empty)** One becomes very dry up here, you know ... the heat from the lights and all this talking ... very dry ... very dry, indeed ... (Keep going until someone offers a drink) Thank you, sir! A gentleman and a boozer! I thought the house had been taken by the Caledonian Society ... of course I only drink to be sociable ... and I'm a *very* sociable chap ...

**(if the Chairman is sent up a pint, he is sometimes instructed by shouts from the donor to down in one. If the Chairman can do so it is always very popular. He can then say with dismay)** Oh, it's empty again ... !

**(if another drink is sent up)** Thank you, sir ... (Toast the donor) What a lovely old custom this is, treating the Chairman ... I do hope it's not dying out ...

Today is Mr Gladstone's birthday. Did you get him anything?

**(after suggestive story)** Good evening, Officer ... I have to be obscene to be believed. My mother told me that one.

Here is an appeal on behalf of the Guild of Distressed Young Gentlewomen ... (Piercing female scream from the rear of the auditorium) ... thank you.

**(if a pretty girl hands the Chairman a prop during the performance, he should wait till she has exited then say)** Chairman's perks ...

**(if coins are thrown on stage during the performance, the Chairman can gather them up and say)** All coins found on stage during the performance are Chairman's perks ...

Here is a short address: Number 3 High Street

I see in the (local paper) that the police are looking for a tall, handsome man for assaulting women. I thought if the money was good I might apply

I see in the (local paper) that the police are looking for a man with one eye called Murphy. I wonder what his other eye's called?

I understand we have in the house tonight a party from (local) ... just paying your respects to civilization?

**or** Just over here to have a bath?

If my old professor could see me now—he'd turn in his gymslip.

I get paid by the laugh—tuppence a titter—so don't suppress it, will you, dear ... no, don't do that—it goes to your thighs ...

**(before Chairman's spot)** And now we come to the Chairman's spot ... I hasten to add this is not a medical term ...

**(after Chairman's act)** Thank you very much ... enough of entertainment, now—on with the show

**(on hot evening)** Any gentleman feeling the heat—and I use the term in the purely English sense of the expression—is at liberty to remove his upper and outer garments. Any lady

## Your Distinguished Chairman 121

feeling warm is at liberty to remove anything . . . (wait for reaction) . . . anything that modesty permits

**(if a portrait of the Queen is displayed, the following can be used after the loyal toast)** Isn't that a magnificent portrait for Her Majesty? It is my own property, as a matter of fact . . . it's an old family heirloom . . . yes, it was handed down to me by my father—he was still on the ladder when the police arrived

Her Majesty was in fact to have been with us tonight—yes, Her Gracious Majesty Queen Victoria in person. Unfortunately she couldn't make it—I understand she's feeling dizzy. (Disraeli —this gag only to be used for specialized houses)

**(to man who has just paid for drinks)** You can tell he's new here— he didn't count his change

**(if a waiter comes to take an order from a party at a table close to the Chairman, it is advisable to wait until the order has been taken or the audience will be very distracted. When this happens, the Chairman can assist with the ordering of drinks by stepping off the stage, going to the table and saying)** That's one gin and tonic here . . . pint of bitter there . . . one Scotch . . . water or soda? . . . (and so on, such as) . . . tomato juice? That won't grow hairs on your chest—oh, it's for you, dear, I'm sorry . . . go on, love—treat yourself to a port and lemon. He's paying. (Then as waiter is going) . . . and I'll have a half of best, thank you, dear/son . . . (then Chairman returns to the podium smugly)

**(During an act in which an artiste is lashing himself or herself into a frenzy, the Chairman can bang his gavel two or three times and say)** Mr/Miss N! Take hold of yourself, please!

**(for opening or closing of show)** I'd like to congratulate the (local) Theatre for their good taste in booking us . . . (For use by visiting company)

**(sports events can be utilized by the Chairman to good effect. If a local soccer team has had a famous victory that afternoon and a party of supporters is in, he can enquire the reason for their high spirits and say)** Oh, how interesting . . . United has won, have they? . . . and who exactly are United . . . oh, a football team . . . I only follow cricket/tiddlywinks myself . . .

**(the rivalry between rugby union and rugby league can sometimes be exploited, and the Chairman can stress his superior breeding)** The only sport I ever played at school was the Wall Game, actually . . .

If the Chairman's family is in the house, it is always a very popular move to introduce them from the stage. The follow-spot can pick them up in the auditorium

(state events can be incorporated into the Chairman's patter) I see Her Majesty's opening Parliament yet again . . . they will keep losing that key . . .

or Well, the elections are upon us again—my vote goes to Mr Disraeli every time—he'll make a wonderful mayor for this town . . . Dead? . . . my newspapers do tend to be delivered late these days . . . or, well that's appropriate isn't it?

(While pattering the Chairman can be folding up a large piece of paper in a very dexterous and significant way. At the conclusion of the patter, he walks back to his table and stuffs the folded wad under one of the legs and then tests to see that the table is no longer wobbling)

The party from (local) during the interval have made me a wonderful presentation, ladies and gentlemen—it is so kind of them —it's in my dressing-room now . . . a giant tin of baked beans . . . I'd just like to say I am deeply moved

(if someone leaves their seat after ten minutes or so) What—had enough already? Coward . . .

or Hello—the critics are in . . .

or Do you know where it is? He'll be back in a wee while . . .

or He's gone to have one on the house . . .

(when the person returns) Hello, all right, now? Could you hear us in there? Yes, we could hear you out here . . .

(when person leaves rather distractingly, the Chairman should keep the patter going at their expense, then when they have finally left the auditorium, say) I thought he'd/she'd never go . . .

(when Chairman is handed a note requesting the removal of a car) I'm afraid we have a slight contretemps in our carriage-park, it would seem. Will the owner of the motorized velocipede, number (give registration number), please move it before it is moved for him . . . they'll never catch on . . .

For wedding anniversaries, the Chairman can offer congratulations and ask the husband for some words on advice on happy marriage for the bachelors present

(for engagements the Chairman can look mournful, place his hand over his heart and offer his deepest commiserations. He then offers sincere congratulations and asks) When is the happy day? (On being told he says) Can we all come?

## Your Distinguished Chairman

**(for a couple who have been married that day)** So what the hell are you doing *here*?

**(if the Chairman has a number of celebrations to deal with he can say)** Anything else being celebrated? Anybody getting divorced Anybody's bath night? (if there is the response "Yes" for the latter the Chairman can say) So that's why you're sitting on your own...

**or** Yes, I could tell from here—you might have had it *before* coming...

**(Where food is being served)** Everything is untouched by human hand—the chef's a gorilla. He can rustle up a steak with his eyes shut—which is the best way to eat it.

Sorry if the service is slow tonight—the chef's off ill. I told him not to eat here.

The food is splendid here. I've been in the kitchen and 20,000 flies can't be wrong.

Don't have the tomato soup—the chef's a vampire

They do marvellous lunches here as well. I had a splendid three-course lunch today—two chips and a pea.

**(To persistent talkers)** I'm sorry—am I interrupting your conversation? OR I'm sorry, I missed that—I was talking.

**(To person arriving with trayful of drinks)** There's my salary on that tray... which is mine?

**(If there is a crash)** And stay out! That's the historical part of the show, folks—the fall of China.

Are there any mother-in-laws in the house!... Oh, good, we can have a hanging!

**(Putting spectacles on)** Sorry about this. I have to wear specs these days—it's my old housemaster's warnings coming home to roost

Ah well, chacun à son gout—that's French for Jack's got the gout.

Ah well, sic transit gloria mundi.-that's Latin for I hope Gloria'll be all right by Monday.

If you have any requests please hand them to me written on a £20 note

Unfortunately N. is unable to be with us tonight—he's/she's helping the police with their enquiries OR he's/she's been refused bail

**(To someone leaving)** I never forget a back... I don't mind 'em going out—it's when they start coming this way I get worried. OR Oh, must you go now? What a shame!

So nice to have seen you ... do come again ... (*ad lib until they have gone*) Oh, I thought he'd/she'd never go

**(To person in front row)** No, don't pick your nose ... please, sir, take your hands out of your pockets and stop counting OR That's a nice turn of leg you've got there madam ... pity it's only the one

I understand we've had complaints about the acoustics. Well, we've put down traps and poison so we're doing our best

Anyone here for (local)? Your coach has gone

Anyone here tonight having their annual do?

**(To party of ladies)** All you girls in the club? I always say that an audience without ladies is like a garden without flowers ... (*wait for "Ahhh!"*) What a creep!

Tonight we have Alec in charge of the lights—Alectrician

**(To person or party which has 'sent up' a straight song)** Thank you, Miss N—battling against the odds ... may I remind you that there are other people in the audience so would you please show more consideration? (*This kind of slap-down ALWAYS elicits a round of applause, but use it sparingly*)

**(To foreigner)** Do you speak English? ... Yes, you look intelligent

### Raffle

When a raffle is to be held the Chairman should announce the fact early in the evening, giving the prices of the tickets, the nature of the prizes, the time of the draw—usually after the interval—and also the title of the organization on whose behalf the raffle is being held. Capital can be sometimes made out of this, i.e. *All the proceeds from the raffle are going to the Charlie Ramsbottom Benevolent Fund*, where Charlie Ramsbottom is the chairman or secretary of the club. As a visitor I usually draw the raffle tickets myself, saving time and fuss, but if a lady in the house has a birthday it is always appreciated if she is asked up (*see following paragraph*)

Your committee has some wonderful prizes for you tonight: see page 64.

### Birthdays

**(to select a member of the audience to make the draw, the Chairman can say)** Have we any young lady in the house tonight celebrating the anniversary of her birthday? ... but then, of course ... all ladies are young ... (If no response ask for a young man.

If still no response select the nearest personable looking female) We'd like you to make the draw for us, my dear—what is your Christian or kosher name . . . well, you never know . . . Janet? Very well, Janet, if you'll kindly step up here we have a little present for you. (Start *"Happy Birthday"*. As Girl reaches stage lead her to the wings evilly. When song is over) There now, I bet you've never been serenaded by five hundred drunks before, have you? All you have to do is to pick a number out of the hat . . . a roll on the drums, please, Maestro (if there is only a pianist) oh, well, do your best . . . pick out a number, Janet . . . (Hold hat up too high for her to reach) I beg your pardon . . . (Call out numbers and distribute prizes. Don't waste time on this—if the winning numbers are not claimed give a "Going, going, gone" with the gavel and pick again. When all the prizes have been given out give the girl a kiss and hand her back to her seat, asking for a round of applause. For prize-winners say) Don't drink it all at once . . .
or I'll be round for my 10 per cent later . . . .
**(for twenty-first birthdays the procedure is much the same, except of course that** *"Twenty-one Today"* **is sung after which the Chairman can say)** Dear me . . . twenty-one today . . . that reminds me of my youth . . . I think he joined the Navy . . .
**(if there is a call for "speech" this should be encouraged. The speech will probably simply be a muttered "Thank you very much", at which the Chairman can say)** . . . well said . . . brief and to the point . . . admirably done . . .

The Chairman would be well advised to establish all the birthdays being celebrated that day, since it is infuriating to sing *"Happy Birthday"* only to have someone else pop up and ask for it to be sung again. It is advisable to ask for all the birthdays of the day, and then sing *"Happy Birthday"* to them all, incorporating all their names in the penultimate line.

Some Chairmen ask for "visitors from abroad" and then proceed to do a virtuoso performance with ready quips for any and all nationalities which are thrown at him. This is fine if the programme is short and contains no patter comedians, and if there is likely to be a variety of nationalities present, but it can get out of hand and go on for a very, very long time. I do not advise this routine for the average Music Hall or the inexperienced Chairman.

If the Chairman is asked to do a Mock Auction—decline. I will say no more than this, with great reluctance I once agreed to conduct one before the performance. It was, as I suspected, a great mistake.

# AUTHOR'S LAST WORD

I would like to think I have covered every eventuality that the Chairman is likely to meet, but I know this is not so and can never be.

So often I have stood in the wings as the overture played and have wondered, "What is going to happen *tonight*? Will I be able to cope? Will I be entertaining? Will I be amusing?" Of course there must be times when one fails to a greater or lesser extent, but I sincerely hope that with the aid of this book the reader will be able to avoid my mistakes, and to profit from my experience.

To be in the Chair for a first-rate Music Hall bill in front of a lively, responsive audience is a challenge which, if met and surmounted, represents one of the most thrilling experiences available to the performer—and I speak as an actor of more than thirty years professional experience.

Unquestionably actors make better chairmen than comics—the actor is not so obsessed with getting laughs and is prepared to play the part of a Victorian or Edwardian dignitary without constantly dropping all pretence of a period style in order to assure us that he is still the same lovable old Jolly Jim we see on television or at our local night-club. The drawbacks to the actor of taking the Chair are that he has neither a set script nor a preconceived character to hide behind; he is solely dependent on his native wit and personality. This book provides the wit—you must find your own personality.

I can promise you that the effort is worth it.

MICHAEL KILGARRIFF

# INDEX OF SONG TITLES

After The Ball, 20
Ain't It Nice?, 33, 38, 78
All The Nice Girls Love A Sailor, 29
And The Great Big Saw Comes Nearer And Nearer, 18
A Bachelor Gay, 34
Bang Went The Chance of a Lifetime, 68
Beer Glorious Beer!, 21
Boiled Beef And Carrots, 21
Burlington Bertie, 87
The Buttercup Song, 18
Caller Herrin', 21
Charming Weather, 22
Come Where The Booze Is Cheaper, 21
Comrades, 12, 17
The Cucumber Song, 21
Daddy Wouldn't Buy Me A Bow-Wow, 78, 82
Daisy Belle, 30, 55
Don't Dilly Dally, 27, 77
Don't Have Anymore, Mrs Moore, 88
Down At The Old Bull And Bush, 30
Drink To Me Only . . ., 21
El Abanico, 22
Eton Boating Song, 22
Excelsior!, 18
The Floral Dance, 32
The Gypsy Warned Me, 87
Happy Birthday, 12, 126
Has Anybody Seen My Tiddler?, 78, 82
Having A Bit Tonight, 21
Hello, Hello, Who's Your Lady Friend?, 12
Here We Are Again, 12, 32

Honeysuckle And The Bee, 8
I Ain't Arf A Lucky Kid, 30
I Do Like An Egg For My Tea, 21
I Do Like To Be Beside The Seaside, 30
If I Should Plant A Tiny Seed Of Love, 34
I Live In Trafalgar Square, 32
I'll Make A Man Of You, 79
I'm 'Enery The Eighth I Am, 37
I'm Going Back To Himazas, 27, 30
I'm Shy, Mary Ellen, I'm Shy, 46
In The Good Old Summertime, 12
I Was A Good Little Girl (Till I Met You), 33, 94
John Willie, Come On, 88
Knees Up Mother Brown, 30
Knocked 'Em In The Old Kent Road (Wot Cher!), 30
The Laughing Song, 32
Let's All Go To The Music Hall, 27
Little Annie Rooney, 18
The Lost Chord, 32
Love's Old Sweet Song, 32
The Marrow Song, 21, 27
Moonstruck, 12, 22
Mother's Advice, 87
Mrs 'Enery 'Awkins, 87
My Hero, 32
My Love Lies Sleeping, 69
Oh, Oh, Antonio, 80
Old Father Thames, 73
My Old Dutch, 68
One Fine Day, 12, 32
On Mother Kelly's Doorstep, 28
On With The Motley, 32, 88
Picking All The Big Ones Out, 21
Pipes Of Pan Are Calling, 18
Row Row Row, 22
Silver Threads Among The Gold, 17
Smilin' Through, 32

Sunshine Of Your Smile, 32
Sweet Rosie O'Grady, 37
Swing Me Higher Obadiah, 78, 82
Ta Ra Ra Boom De Ay, 65, 82
Tell Me Pretty Maiden, 18
Tenor and Baritone, 18
There Was I Waiting At The Church, 28
Turned Up, 69
Twenty-One Today, 12, 126
Vilia, 32
Voi Che Sapete, 32

Wait Till The Clouds Roll By, 17
What I Want Is A Proper Cup Of Coffee, 21
When I Take My Morning Promenade, 78
Where Did You Get That Hat?, 12
While Strolling Through The Park, 17
White Wings, 17
Who Were You With Last Night?, 80
Why Am I Always The Bridesmaid?, 78
Women, 22

www.ingramcontent.com/pod-product-compliance
Ingram Content Group UK Ltd.
Pitfield, Milton Keynes, MK11 3LW, UK
UKHW021842140426

5217IPUK00022B/1547